XIX BOOKS

ponchos
&wraps
- a Knitter's dozen

Ponchos & Wraps; A Knitter's dozen PUBLISHED BY XRX BOOKS

Credits

PUBLISHER
Alexis Yiorgos Xenakis

MANAGING EDITOR
David Xenakis

COEDITORS
Rick Mondragon
Elaine Rowley

EDITORIAL ASSISTANT
Sue Nelson

INSTRUCTION EDITOR
Joni Coniglio

INSTRUCTION ASSISTANT
Cole Kelley

COPY EDITOR
Holly Brunner

GRAPHIC DESIGNER
Bob Natz

PHOTOGRAPHER
Alexis Xenakis

SECOND PHOTOGRAPHER
Mike Winkleman

STYLIST
Rick Mondragon

PRODUCTION DIRECTOR &
COLOR SPECIALIST
Dennis Pearson

BOOK PRODUCTION
MANAGER
Susan Becker

PRODUCTION
Everett Baker
Nancy Holzer

TECHNICAL ILLUSTRATIONS
Jay Reeve
Carol Skallerud

SPECIAL ILLUSTRATIONS
Natalie Sorenson

MIS
Jason Bittner

FIRST PUBLISHED IN USA IN 2005 BY XRX, INC.

ISBN 1-933064-01-3
Produced in Sioux Falls, South Dakota, by XRX, Inc.,
PO Box 1525, Sioux Falls, SD 57101-1525 USA 605.338.2450

a publication of **XRX** BOOKS

Visit us online at www.knittinguniverse.com

XRX BOOKS

ponchos
&wraps
- a Knitter's dozen

photography by
Alexis Xenakis

1

Friller

2

Paradoxical Poncho

3

Cape Pointe

4

All-Seasons Poncho

5

Waterfalls

6

Petal Power

ponchos & wraps

12

Anthracite Shawl

13

Dappled Capelet

14

Sugarplum & Toffee

15

Rhythm and Blues

16

Dramatic Datewear

17

Trapezoid Ruana

- a Knitter's dozen CONTENTS

v

Welcome

A poncho or other wrap is a most forgiving layer. It is ready to be thick and warm or light and airy; to look glamorous or casual, elegant or irreverent; to envelope or skim. What else can be worn front to back, even front (or back) to side? What else allows such a range of expression—from decisive fling to dreamy whirl? It has few issues—no sleeves to squeeze other sleeves into, no hemline to place advantageously (or at least not un-advantageously)—and when you are knitting one, very few AT SAME TIME's.

When we first think about knitting a wrap, we relax into an expansive, idea-generating mode. The shape is simple, fit is rarely an issue, gauge is not critical. The canvas is large and does not confine. The knitting is irresistible. It's comfort knitting.

So, although this book began as a collection of 12 designs from past issues of *Knitter's Magazine*, we were soon up to our needles in yarns and inspiration. Planning and knitting answers to 'What if...?' While most appear here as Make it Yours! additions to other designs, a few are new, and more wait to be knit.

We know you too will find favorites and wonder 'what if I made it in ribbon?... in this stunning hand-paint mohair...?' All that's required is getting the fabric right. For this, take time to make an ample swatch (at least 6–8" square) and wash or steam it well. * If you don't love it, try another, changing needle size, stitch, yarn, color, or color sequence—then compare. Repeat from * until you do love it. You'll have a unique wrap and a bonus—the confidence that comes from making it yours! Soon your knitter's dozen, like ours, will grow to twenty-something... or more.

Throughout this book, the yarns are described generically and the specific yarn is listed with each photograph. Some of the yarns are no longer available, but may live on in our memories and stashes.

Sometimes working with the yarn is all that's needed. From a keep-it-so-simple neckline to an indestructible loop fringe, this layer packs attitude.

Designed by Sue Kay Nelson

Friller

EASY

One Size

10cm/4"

28

20

• over stockinette stitch
(knit on RS, purl on WS)

1 2 3 **4** 5 6

• Medium weight
• 830 yds

• 4.5mm/US7, or size to obtain gauge,
60 cm (24") long

• 5mm/H-8

Notes

1 See *Techniques*, page 80, for SSK, and single crochet. **2** The neck edges have no shaping. When joined, a V-neck forms.

STOCKINETTE VARIATION

Work smooth sections of the yarn in stockinette stitch (k on RS, p on WS) and bouclé (loopy) sections in reverse stockinette stitch (p on RS, k on WS), changing stitch pattern whenever the yarn changes—even mid-row.

Back

Cast on 4 sts.
Work in Stockinette Variation AT SAME TIME shaping the poncho as follows:
Rows 1 and 3 (WS) Work even.
Row 2 Work 1 st, knit in the front and back of the next stitch (kf&b) twice, work 1 st.
Row 4 Work 1 st, kf&b, work to last 2 sts, kf&b, work 1 st. Repeat Rows 3 and 4 until there are 200 sts on needle, ending with a WS row.
Divide for neck: Next row Work 85 sts, bind off 30 sts, work to end.
Work Left Front
Row 1 (WS) Work 85 sts, turn work.
Row 2 Work to last 3 sts, k2tog, work last st.

Row 3 Work even. Work Rows 2 and 3 for 7", ending with a WS row. Break yarn.
Work Right Front
With WS facing, join second ball of yarn at neck edge.
Row 1 (WS) Work 85 sts.
Row 2 Work 1 st, SSK, work to end.
Row 3 Work even. Work Rows 2 and 3 for 7", ending with a WS row. Do not break yarn.
Join Fronts
Work across all stitches as follows:
RS rows Work 1 st, SSK, work to last 3 sts of Left Front, k2tog, work 1 st.
WS rows Work even. Repeat last two rows until 4 sts remain. Bind off.

Crochet loop fringe
Neckline
Row 1 Starting at shoulder, work single crochet (sc) around neckline, join last st to first st.
Row 2 * Chain 20, skip 1 sc, sc in next st; repeat from * around. Fasten off.
Lower edge
Starting at back point of poncho, attach yarn, * chain 20, skip 1 row, sc in next row, repeat from * around.

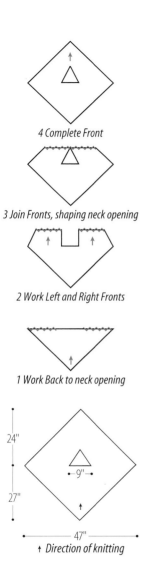

4 Complete Front

3 Join Fronts, shaping neck opening

2 Work Left and Right Fronts

1 Work Back to neck opening

24"

27"

←—9"—→

47"

↑ Direction of knitting

DIAKEITO Diadrey
(54% mohair, 38% wool,
8% nylon; 40g/1.4oz;
83m/91yds) in color 206

Gitta fashioned this elegant poncho from two identical pieces of knitting. The paradox? Each piece is half of the front and half of the back. This allows partial front and back seams to end in pairs of tassels.

Designed by Gitta Schrade

Paradoxical Poncho

it's easy
...go
for it!

EASY +

S/M (L/1X)
Finished measurements
Widest point 36 (43)"
Length at center seam 25 (27)"

10cm/4"

34
18
• over garter stitch (knit every row) using larger needles

1 2 3 **4** 5 6

• Medium weight
• 1200 (1500) yds

• 4.5mm/US7, or size to obtain gauge

• 4mm/US6, 40 cm/16" long

&

• stitch markers

Notes

1 See *Techniques*, page 80, for yarn over (yo), tassels, and mattress stitch. **2** Poncho is worked from the top down. Neckband is worked circularly and body is worked back and forth in rows, working right and left halves of body separately.

Neckband

With circular needle, cast on 104 (112) sts. Place marker (pm) and join, being careful not to twist stitches.
Round 1 * K2, p2; repeat from *.
Repeat Round 1 until piece measures 6".

Right half of body

Change to larger needles and remove marker.
Row 1 (RS) K1, p1, k1, pm, k22 (24), pm, k2 (shoulder), pm, k22 (24), pm, k1, p1, k1. Leave remaining 52 (56) sts on circular needle for left half. Turn work.
Row 2 (WS) P1, k1, p1, knit to last 3 sts, p1, k1, p1.
Row 3 K1, p1, k1, slip marker (sm), yo, knit to next marker, yo, sm, k2, sm, yo, knit to next marker, yo, sm, k1, p1, k1—56 (60) sts.

Row 4 Repeat Row 2.
Keeping first and last 3 sts of every row in rib as established and all other stitches in garter stitch, continue to work a yo before and after shoulder markers on every RS row 7 (10) times more, AT SAME TIME, continue to work a yo after first marker and before last marker every 3rd row (alternately every 2nd row once, every 3rd row once) until piece measures 19 (20)" from last shoulder increase. Bind off.

Left half of body

With larger needles, work 52 (56) sts on hold as for right half.

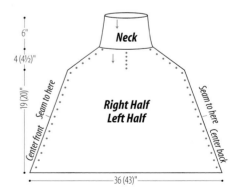

6"
4 (4½)"
19 (20)"
Neck
Center front
Seam to here
Right Half
Left Half
Seam to here
center back
36 (43)"

Finishing

Block pieces. Sew pieces together at front and back, using mattress stitch, working a half stitch in from each edge, and ending 11" from bound-off edge. Fold neckband in half to wrong side and sew in place.

Tassels

Make 6 tassels, 5" long. Using photo as guide, sew 1 tassel to each point at lower edge of front and back. Sew 2 tassels to center front below neckband.

NATURALLY Natural Wool Aran 10-Ply (100% wool; 200g/7oz; 341m/379yds) in Brown Gray

If luscious wool doesn't ward off the chills, the beautiful kettle-dyed colors will. This easy-knit cape deserves distinctive buttons to keep it in place as you go about your day. Wear it as a wrap or over your coat for added warmth.

Designed by Kathy Cheifetz

Cape Pointe

EASY

One size
Finished measurements
Length 41" • Width 86"

10cm/4"

24

14

• over garter stitch (knit every row)

1 2 3 4 **5** 6

• Bulky weight
A • 490 yds, B • 340 yds
C • 190 yds, D • 135 yds

• 6.5mm/US10½, or size to obtain gauge,
100cm/40" long

• 6mm/J-10

• six 24mm/1"

&

• stitch marker

4

Notes
1 See *Techniques*, page 80, for crochet chain (ch). **2** Slip stitches knitwise with yarn in back.

Stripe pattern
6 rows A, 8 rows B, 6 rows A, 8 rows D, 6 rows A, 8 rows B, 6 rows A, 8 rows C. Repeat these 56 rows for stripe pattern.

CAPE
With A, cast on 6 sts.
Begin stripe pattern and shaping: Row 1 (RS) K6.
Row 2 Slip 1 (sl 1), knit into front and back of next stitch (kf&b), k4—7 sts.
Row 3 Sl 1, kf&b, k5—8 sts.
Row 4 Sl 1, kf&b, k1, [kf&b] twice, k3—11 sts.
Row 5 Sl 1, kf&b, k9—12 sts.
Row 6 Sl 1, kf&b, k3, [kf&b] twice, k5—15 sts.
Row 7 With B, sl 1, kf&b, k13—16 sts.
Row 8 Sl 1, kf&b, k5, kf&b, place marker, kf&b, k7—19 sts.
Row 9 Sl 1, kf&b, knit to end.
Row 10 Sl 1, kf&b, knit to 1 st before marker, kf&b, slip marker, kf&b, knit to end. Repeat Rows 9 and 10 for shaping, and continue in stripe pattern

as established until 56 rows of stripe pattern have been worked 3 times, then work first 19 rows once more (187 rows total)—376 sts. Bind off.

Closure loops *(make 3)*
With crochet hook, ch 10, sl st to first chain to close loop, then ch 10 more and sl st to first loop to make a figure-8.

Finishing
With a steam iron and pressing cloth, gently steam the slip-stitch edges (this relaxes the fronts and allows the cape to hang straight). Sew 3 buttons on each front in desired positions, using photo as guide. Attach center of closure loops to right front. If desired, fold edge at back neck down to form a collar.

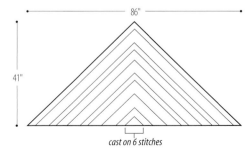

MANOS DEL URUGUAY *Hand-dyed Pure Wool (100% wool; 100g/3½oz; 126m/138yds) in Prairie (A), Bing Cherry (B), Brick (C), and Topaz (D)*

Comfortable and easy to wear, the poncho matches just about any outfit. A poncho can be worn with the point in front and back, or like a raglan with the front and back squared off. Knit seamlessly from the neck down, this poncho works up quickly and effortlessly, with just enough 2-color work to be interesting.

Designed by Mary Rich Goodwin

All-Seasons Poncho

INTERMEDIATE

S (M, L, 1X)
Finished measurements
Circumference 122 (133, 139, 150)"
Length 24½ (27, 28, 30¼)"

10cm/4"

22 … 18

• over stockinette stitch (knit every round)
using larger needle and MC

1 2 3 **4** 5 6

• Medium weight
MC • 800 (800, 1000, 1200) yds
A, B, C • 400 yds each

• 5.5mm/US9, or size to obtain gauge,
60cm/24" and 100cm/40" long
• 4mm/US6, 40cm/16" long

&

• four stitch markers

Notes
1 See *Techniques*, page 80, for SSK.
2 Poncho is worked circularly from the neck down. **3** When working increases in chart pattern, knit into front and back of stitch with next chart color, then continue with pattern (you will have 2 stitches of the same color). **4** Change to longer circular needle when necessary.

Rib Pattern
Rounds 1, 3, 5, and 6 * K2, p2; repeat from *.
Rounds 2 and 4 * K2tog, do not slip off needle, knit first stitch again, slip both stitches off needle, p2; repeat from *.

PONCHO
With smaller needle and MC, cast on 108 (120, 120, 132) sts. Place marker (pm) and join, being careful not to twist stitches. Knit 8 rounds. Work 6 rounds of Rib Pattern. Change to larger (24") needle.
Begin Chart A: Round 1 Work 3-st repeat of Chart around.
Round 2 (increase round) With A, slip marker, * knit into front and back of stitch (kf&b), k25 (28, 28, 31), kf&b, pm; repeat from *, ending at round marker— 29 (32, 32, 35) sts between markers.

Round 3 Knit.
Round 4 * Kf&b, knit to 1 stitch before marker, kf&b; repeat from *. Work patterns and increases simultaneously as follows:
Work 13 rounds Chart B, 7 rounds with MC, 30 rounds Chart C, 33 (43, 49, 59) rounds with MC, 17 rounds Chart D, AT SAME TIME, work increases as established before and after each marker (8 sts increased) every other round—131 (144, 150, 163) sts between markers.

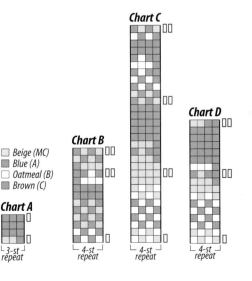

Chart C

Chart D

□ Beige (MC)
■ Blue (A)
□ Oatmeal (B)
■ Brown (C)

Chart B

Chart A

└ 3-st ┘ repeat   └ 4-st ┘ repeat   └ 4-st ┘ repeat   └ 4-st ┘ repeat

PLYMOUTH Encore Colorspun (75% acrylic, 25% wool; 100g/3½oz; 180m/200yds) in Beige (MC); Encore Worsted (75% acrylic, 25% wool; 100g/3½oz; 200m/220yds) Brown (A), Oatmeal (B), Denim Blue (C)

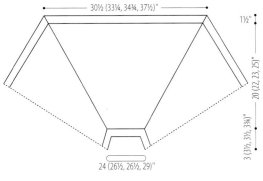

30½ (33¼, 34¾, 37½)"

1½"

20 (22, 23, 25)"

3 (3½, 3½, 3¾)"

24 (26½, 26½, 29)"

Begin Rib Pattern: Next round * K2 C, p2 MC; repeat from *. Continue in pattern through Round 6, AT SAME TIME, continue increases as established—137 (150, 156, 169) sts between markers. Bind off in pattern. Block piece.

8

5

Waterfalls ▶

5

Waterfalls

Ladder stitch is an ideal choice to showcase the beauty of hand-dyed yarns. We knit a long and loose muffler in garter stitch, then dropped a few stitches to create a wider, lacy-look shawl. It was so much fun that we made 6 more variations. The only secret to knitting this beauty is the cast-on and bind-off treatment.

Designed by Knitter's Design Team

EASY +

Six variations, One size each

Finished measurements
See captions for individual waterfall measurements

10cm/4"

32

16

• over garter stitch
(knit every row)
with A and B held together

1 2 3 4 **5** 6

• Bulky weight
• Equal yardages of A and B, see captions for specifics

• 6mm/US10, or size to obtain gauge

• small amount of waste yarn for cast-on

Note

1 See *Techniques*, page 80, for knit through back loop.

WATERFALL CAST-ON

With waste yarn, cast on required number of stitches. Knit 2 rows. Change to shawl yarns and knit 1 row.
Next row Knit every stitch through the back loop.

THE BASICS

Cast on __ sts (a multiple of 7 + 5) with Waterfall Cast-on. With A and B held together, knit to desired length. Bind off with Waterfall Bind-off. Block.

WATERFALL BIND-OFF

Bind off 4 sts,* remove loop from right-hand needle and pull skein of yarn through loop (illustration 1), knit next 2 sts (illustration 2), bind off next 4 sts; repeat from * to end. You now have 4 pairs of stitches surrounded by 5-stitch–wide bound-off panels. Remove needles and drop the paired stitches down to the cast-on edge (illustration 3). Snip a waste yarn stitch and remove waste yarn.

WATERFALL BIND-OFF

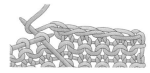

1 Bind off 4 stitches, then pull working yarn through loop.

2 Knit next 2 stitches. Repeat steps 1 and 2 across piece, ending bind off 4 stitches.

3 Remove needle, drop the paired stitches down to the cast-on edge, forming ladders.

it's easy ...go for it!

10

FIESTA La Luz (100% silk; 60g/2oz; 192m/210yds) in Amador (A);
La Boheme 2-strand yarn (64% mohair, 28% wool, 8% nylon/100%
rayon boucle; 116g/4oz; 150m/165yds) in Moroccan (B); 290 yds each

GOLD STOLE
Follow The Basics, casting on 33 sts (for 13½"
finished width) and knitting 92".

RED STOLE
Follow The Basics, casting on 47 sts (for 19½"
finished width) and knitting 70".

La Luz in 3307 Cherry (A)
La Boheme in 11214 Poppies (B); 400 yds each

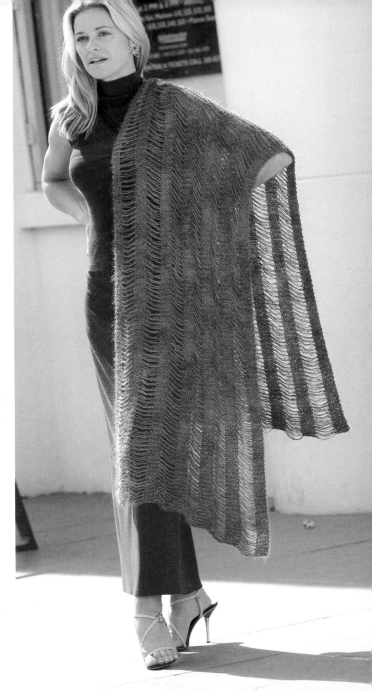

Make it Yours!

DENIM STOLE

Follow The Basics (page 10), casting on 33 sts (for 13" finished width) and knitting 76".

BERROCO Suede (100% nylon; 50g/1¾oz; 111m/120yds) in Hopalong Cassidy (A)
SKACEL Tropicana (100% nylon; 50g/1¾oz; 50m/55yds) in Blues and Almond 304 (B); 330 yds each

BEIGE SCARF

Follow The Basics (page 10), EXCEPT for this narrow scarf, use a multiple of 5 + 3. Cast on 13 sts (for 5½" finished width). Knit 84".
Then work Waterfall Bind-off EXCEPT * bind off 2 sts, knit 2; repeat from *, end bind off 2.

La Luz in Champagne (A)
La Boheme in Painted Desert (B); 170 yds each

The Waterfall Corner

1 Knit to desired length, ending with a WS row.

2 First stairstep section
* Knit to last 7 stitches, turn and knit back; repeat from * 4 more times (5 ridges).

Second stairstep section
* Knit to last 14 stitches, turn and knit back; repeat from * 4 more times (5 ridges).

Third and fourth sections
Continue, working each 10-row section over 7 fewer stitches, until last section has only 5 stitches.

3 Corner Section
Work 20 rows (10 ridges) on 5 stitches.

4 Then work 10-row stairstep section over 7 more stitches.

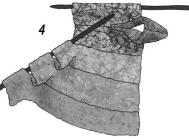

5 Continue, working each 10-row section over 7 more stitches until last section is worked over all stitches. Work even to next corner or bind-off.

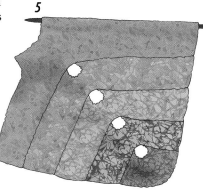

Stairstep Sections

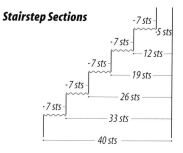

-7 sts / 5 sts
-7 sts / 12 sts
-7 sts / 19 sts
-7 sts / 26 sts
-7 sts / 33 sts
40 sts

4-Corner Collar

With waste yarn, cast on 40 sts (a multiple of 7 + 5). Knit 2 rows. Change to main yarn and knit 6" (or desired length to first corner), ending with a WS row. Work Waterfall Corner (page 14). * Knit 6" (to next corner) then work Waterfall Corner; repeat from * 2 more times. Do not bind off. (If using 'Touch Me,' place stitches on hold and see note below.) Drop stitches as follows: * Slip 5, drop 2; repeat from *, ending slip 5. Graft last row to first row of main yarn (see grafting garter stitch, page 82) as follows: * Graft 5 sts, skip float; repeat from * across, ending graft 5 sts. Snip a waste yarn stitch, remove waste yarn, and steam.

Touch Me Note
When using 'Touch Me,' it is necessary to machine wash (warm water, gentle cycle) and machine dry (warm) the piece before dropping stitches.

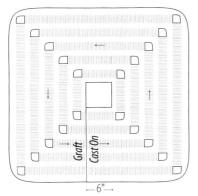

MUENCH Touch Me (72% rayon, 28% wool; 50g/1¾oz; 56m/60yds) in Amador; 275 yds (single strand used)

V-Shawl

Cast on 40 sts (a multiple of 7 + 5) with Waterfall Cast-on (page 10).

1 Knit to corner (desired length or 36"), ending with a WS row.

2 *First stairstep section* * Knit to last 7 sts, turn and knit back; repeat from * 4 more times (5 ridges).

Second stairstep section * Knit to last 14 sts, turn and knit back; repeat from * 4 more times (5 ridges).

Third and fourth stairstep sections Continue, working each 10-row stairstep section over 7 fewer stitches until last section has only 5 stitches.

3 *Corner section* Work 20 rows (10 ridges) on 5 stitches.

4 Then work longer 10-row stairstep sections each over 7 more stitches.

5 Repeat Step 4 until working over all stitches.

Knit 36".

Bind off with Waterfall Bind-off (page 10).

Finishing

Unravel stitches and block to size.

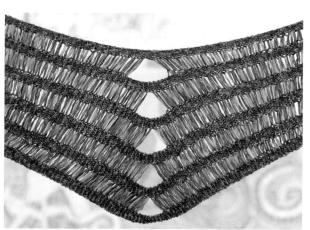

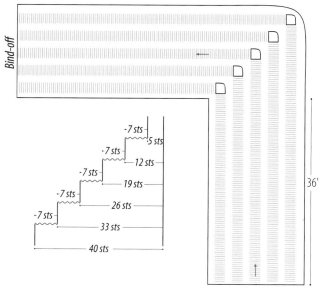

di.VÉ Orientale (97% nylon, 3% polyester 50g/1¾oz; 55m/61yds) in 34325; 600 yds (single strand used)

A vision of curve and color inspired this poncho. Rick rounded the tops of half the blocks and the poncho's silhouette with decreases worked every row. The colorplay is irresistible—imagine a palette of bleached grays and tans or ....

Designed by Rick Mondragon

Petal Power

INTERMEDIATE +

One Size
26" long, 80" circumference
at widest point

10cm/4"

32

18
• over stockinette stitch
(knit on RS, purl on WS)

1 2 3 **4** 5 6

• Medium weight
A, B, C • 190 yds each
D, E • 120 yds each
F, H • 90 yds each
G • 140 yds
I, J, L • 70 yds each
K • 110 yds

• 4mm/US6, or size to obtain gauge,
40 cm (16") long

&

• stitch markers

18

NOTES: 1 See *Techniques*, page 80, for SSK and p2tog. **2** In these instructions, "pick up" means "pick up and knit." Pick up all stitches with RS facing and as indicated on Map. **3** Poncho is worked in Tiers of blocks from hemline to neck opening. Each Tier is made of one block shape (Basic or Modified) in two, alternating colorways. **4** Follow Map on page 21 for color placement. Each Block in Tiers 1–8 is worked in 3 colors. The number of rows worked in each color changes from Tier to Tier. Tier 9 Blocks are worked in 2 colors; Tier 10 Blocks in a single color. Each color change is followed with a wrong-side knit row to form a purl ridge.

Basic Block
Note Tiers 2, 4, 7, 9, and 10 are made of Basic Blocks.
Row 1 (RS) Pick up half the sts along left edge of a previous tier's block, place marker (pm), pick up remaining sts along right edge of next block.
Row 2 and first WS row after each color change Knit.
All other RS rows Knit to 2 sts before marker, SSK, slip marker (sm), k2tog, knit to end—2 sts decreased.
All other WS rows Purl.
When 4 sts remain, break yarn and pull tail through all 4 sts.

Modified Block
Note Tiers 1, 3, 5, 6, and 8 are made of Modified Blocks.
Work all RS rows and WS rows through first WS row of 3rd color as Basic Block.
All remaining WS rows Purl to 2 sts before marker, SSP (see page 21), sm, p2tog, purl to end.
When 4 sts remain, fasten off as usual.

Poncho
Tier 1, Modified 52-st Block
Note Work 5 blocks with colors A, D, and I and 5 blocks with colors J, K, and B.
Row 1 With A or J, cast on 26 sts, pm, cast on 26 more sts.

ROWAN
Yorkshire Tweed dk (100% wool; 50g/1¾oz; 113m/123yds) 349 Frog (A), 344 Scarlet (B), 348 Lime Leaf (C)
Rowanspun dk (100% wool; 50g/1¾oz; 200m/219yds) 735 Eau de Nil (D), 747 Catkin (E), 731 Punch (F), 734 Cloud (G), 736 Goblin (H)
Felted Tweed (50% wool, 25% alpaca, 25% viscose; 50g/1¾oz; 175m/191yds) 146 Herb (I), 152 Watery (J), 154 Pickle (K), 155 Ginger (L)

3 Completed block from Tier 2.

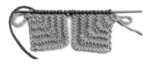

2 Joining blocks of Tier 1 by picking up stitches for Tier 2.

1 One finished block from Tier 1.

Rows 2, 16, 32 (WS) Knit.

Odd rows 3–39 Knit to 2 sts before marker, SSK, sm, k2tog, knit to end, changing to D or K on Row 15 and I or B on Row 31.

Even rows 4–14 Purl.

Even rows 18–30 Purl.

Even rows 34–40 Purl to 2 sts before marker, p2tog, SSP, purl to end.

Row 41 K1, SSK, k2tog, k1. Fasten off 4 sts.

Tier 2, Basic 42-st Block

* Begin Block E-F-K: Row 1 (RS) With E, pick up 21 sts along left edge of a Tier 1 Block J-K-B (see Map), pm, pick up 21 sts along right edge of a Block A-D-I (see illustration 2).

Rows 2, 12, 22 Knit.

Odd rows 3–39 Knit to 2 sts before marker, SSK, sm, k2tog, knit to end, changing to F on Row 11 and K on Row 21.

Even rows 4–10, 14–20, 24–40 Purl. Fasten off 4 sts.

Begin Block C-I-L: Row 1 With C, pick up 21 sts along left edge of same Block A-D-I, pm, pick up 21 sts along right edge of another Block J-K-B. Work as Block E-F-K EXCEPT change to I on Row 11 and L on Row 21. Repeat from * 4 more times—all Tier 1 blocks are joined into a circle.

Continue to alternate colors of blocks as shown on Map on subsequent tiers:

Tier 3, 42-st Modified Block

Work Modified Block, beginning with H or G, changing to D or B on Row 13 and to E or C on Row 27.

Tier 4, 36-st Basic Block

Work Basic Block, beginning with L or K, changing to I or F on Row 13 and to J or G on Row 25.

Tier 5, 36-st Modified Block

Work Modified Block, beginning with B or A, changing to C or D on Row 13 and to H or E on Row 25.

Tier 6, 30-st Modified Block

Work Modified Block, beginning with J or E, changing to K or F on Row 11 and to D or C on Row 21.

Tier 7, 26-st Basic Block

Work Basic Block, beginning with G or I, changing to L or H on Row 11 and to C or B on Row 19.

Tier 8, 24-st Modified Block

Work Modified Block, beginning with E or K, changing to D or J on Row 9 and to F or A on Row 17.

Tier 9, 22-st Basic Block

Work Basic Block, beginning with L or G, changing to I or B on Row 9.

Tier 10, 20-st Basic Block

Row 1 (RS) With C or J, pick up 10 sts, pm, pick up 10 sts.

Row 2 Knit.

All other RS rows K1, SSK, knit to 2 sts before marker, SSK, sm, k2tog, knit to last 3 sts, k2tog, k1.

All other WS rows Purl.

When 4 sts remain, fasten off as usual.

Neckband (Worked in rounds)
With J, pick up 100 sts around neckline
edge of Tier 10, join.
Round 1 Purl.
Next 6 rounds Knit.
Next round With C, knit.
Next round Purl.
Next 6 rounds Knit.
Next round With B, knit.
Bind off in purl.

Color key

- A
- B
- C
- D
- E
- F
- G
- H
- I
- J
- K
- L

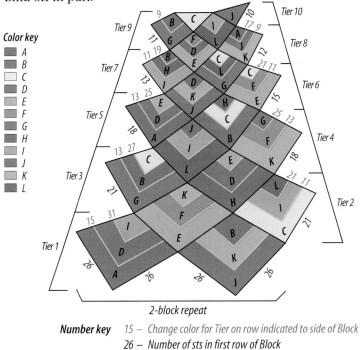

Number key   15 – *Change color for Tier on row indicated to side of Block*
26 – *Number of sts in first row of Block*

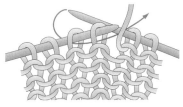

SSP

1 Slip 2 stitches separately to right
needle as if to knit.
2 Slip these 2 stitches back onto left
needle. Insert right needle through
their 'back loops,' into the second
stitch and then the first (see above)
and purl them together.

This lightweight poncho is formed of mitered squares turned on point to form diamonds. Knit four for the front and four for the back. Squares are joined at the sides with 3-needle bind-off.

Designed by Dee Jones

Silk Road

Notes 1 See *Techniques*, page 80, for SSK and 3-needle bind-off. **2** In these instructions, "pick up" means "pick up and knit". Pick up all stitches with RS facing. **3** Refer to the Map, page 23, for placement of Mitered Squares, direction of work, and edges to be sewn.

Basic Mitered Square
Row 1 With A, cast on (or pick up, depending on where you are on the Map) 32 sts, place marker (pm), cast on or pick up 32 more sts.
Row 2 (WS) Knit.
Row 3 With B, knit to 2 sts before marker, k2tog, slip marker (sm), SSK, knit to end.
Row 4 Purl.
Row 5 With A, knit to 2 sts before marker, k2tog, sm, SSK, knit to end.
Row 6 Knit.
Repeat Rows 3–6 until 2 sts remain and you are ready to start a RS row.
Next row K2tog.
Basic Mitered Square measures approximately 10" when joined to other squares.

Front
Beginning with Square 1 and following the numbers on the Map, work Basic Mitered Squares 1–3.
Square 4: Work as Basic Mitered Square until 32 sts remain. With B, bind off loosely.

Back
Work as for Front.

Finishing
Block pieces.
Join Front to Back
With RS facing, and B, pick up a total of 50 sts along Squares 4 and 2 of Front. Cut yarn, leaving sts on needle. With separate needle, RS facing and B, pick up a total of 50 sts along Squares 3 and 4 of Back. Join using 3-needle bind-off. Repeat for other side (joining Squares 4 and 3 of Front to Squares 4 and 2 of Back).

HIMALAYA *Recycled Silk (100% silk; 100g/3½oz; 73m/80yds) in multi (A);* TAHKI *Cotton Classic (100% cotton; 50g/1¾oz; 100m/110yds) in 3994 Deep Red (B)*

8"

4½"

21"

4

2   3

1

Key
────── Cast-on
- - - - - Pick up and knit
wwwww Seam
──────► Direction of knitting

Such a simple concept: Work flat rounds (increasing 8 stitches every other round) from neck opening to shoulders or a bit beyond. Add mitered squares or rectangles for contour, then complete with flat rounds.

Designed by Knitter's Design Team

Another Turn

INTERMEDIATE

37" across
at widest point, 25" long

10cm/4"

28

14
• over Garter Ridge Pattern

1 2 3 6

• Medium to Bulky
Tawny Poncho: MC • 600 yds
CC • a total of 600 yds
Mohair Poncho: 1050 yds

• 5.5mm/US9, or size to obtain gauge
74 cm/29" long
• Second circular needle of same size for
squares and rectangles

&

• stitch markers and holders

Notes
1 See *Techniques*, page 80, for SSK and loop cast-on. **2** In these instructions, "pick up" means "pick up and knit." Pick up all stitches with RS facing and MC. **3** Refer to the Map on pages 26 and 27 for placement of Mitered Squares and direction of work. **4** Poncho is worked in one piece from neck opening down.

Garter Ridge Pattern
Rounds 1, 2 With MC, knit.
Round 3 With CC, knit.
Round 4 With CC, purl.
Repeat Rounds 1–4 for pattern.

Basic Mitered Square
Row 1 With second needle and MC, cast on (pick up, or knit, depending on where you are on the Map) 25 sts, place marker (pm), cast on or pick up 25 more sts.
Row 2 (WS) Purl.
Row 3 With CC, knit to 2 sts before marker, k2tog, SSK, knit to end.
Row 4 Knit.
Row 5 With MC, repeat Row 3.

Row 6 Purl.
Repeat Rows 3–6 until 2 sts remain.
Next row (RS) K2tog, fasten off.
Basic Mitered Square measures approximately 6¾" when joined to other squares.

TAWNY PONCHO
Yoke
With MC, * loosely cast on 22 sts, place marker; repeat from * 3 more times—88 sts. Join and knit 1 round.
Begin Garter Ridge Pattern, increasing on rounds 1 and 3 as follows: * K1, loop cast on 1 st, k to 1 st before next marker, loop cast on 1 st, k1; repeat from * to end. **2** Knit. **4** Purl.
Repeat last 4 rounds, changing CC colors each repeat, for a total of 7 CC ridges—50 sts between markers.

Mitered Squares
Beginning with Square 1 and following the numbers on the Map, work Basic Mitered Squares, using one CC color for each square.

COLINETTE *Tagliatelli* (90% wool, 10% nylon; 100g/3½oz; 145m/160yds) in caramel multicolor (MC) 4 CC yarns used: *Prism, Skye, Wigwam,* and *Zanziba*

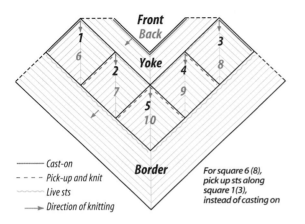

Cast-on —————
Pick-up and knit - - - -
Live sts ～～～～
Direction of knitting ——→

Front
Back
Yoke
1 6 2 7 3 8 4 9 5 10

Border

For square 6 (8),
pick up sts along
square 1 (3),
instead of casting on

Border

With MC, pick up sts as follows: 75 sts along Squares 1, 2 and one side of 5, pm; 75 sts along other side of 5, 4, and 3; 75 sts along 6, 7, and one side of 10, pm; 75 sts along other side of 10, 9 and 8—300 sts. Join and mark beginning of round.

Next (increase) round With MC, * k to 1 st before next marker, loop cast on 1 st, k2, loop cast on 1 st; repeat from *, k to end of round—4 sts increased.

Next round Knit.

Next round With CC, work increase round.

Next round Purl.

Next round With MC, knit.

Repeat last 5 rounds 7 times more—364 sts.

With MC, work increase round, knit 1 round.

Make it Yours!

RED MOHAIR VERSION

Note One yarn is used throughout:
For MC, use a single strand of mohair; for CC, use a double strand of mohair.

Basic Mitered Rectangle 1 (4)

Row 1 With second needle and MC, cast on (for Rectangle 1) or pick up (for Rectangle 4) 25 sts, pm, k50 sts from yoke.

Continue as for Basic Mitered Square until 1 st remains before marker. **Next row** (RS) K3tog, k to end. Place sts on hold.

Basic Mitered Rectangle 2 (5)

Row 1 With second needle and MC, k50 sts from yoke, pm, cast on (for Rectangle 2) or pick up (for Rectangle 5) 25 sts.

Continue as for Basic Mitered Square until 1 st remains after marker. ***Next row*** (RS) Knit to 2 sts before marker, k3tog. Place sts on hold.

Yoke

Work as for Tawny Poncho.

Mitered Rectangles and Squares

Beginning with Rectangle 1 and following the numbers on the Map, work Basic Mitered Rectangles and Squares (see page 24).

Border

With MC pick up sts as follows:

75 sts along Rectangle 1 and one side of Square 3, pm; 75 sts along other side of 3 and Rectangle 2; 75 sts along Rectangle 4 and one side of Square 6, pm; 75 sts along other side of 6 and Rectangle 5—300 sts.

Continue as for Tawny poncho.

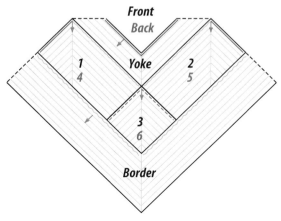

KARABELLA *Gossamer (52% Nylon, 30% Mohair, 18% Polyester; 50g/1¾oz; 200m/222 yds) in 6350 Red/Gold*

The knitting for this wrap starts at the neck edge and increases at the corners on every right-side row. By the time you get to the end, you are working with a lot of stitches—you really need that 40" needle! The pattern is easy to memorize, making it a great take-along project.

Designed by Linda Cyr

Lace in Garter

INTERMEDIATE +

One size
Finished measurements
14" wide × 36" long

10cm/4"

32
18
• over Lace Chart

1 2 3 **4** 5 6

• Medium weight
• 1170 yds

• 4mm/US6, or size to obtain gauge,
100cm/40" long

• stitch markers

Notes

1 See *Techniques*, page 80, for SSK and tassels. *2* Wrap is worked from the neck edge out.

WRAP

Cast on 266 sts. Knit 4 rows.
Begin Lace Chart: Row 1 (RS) K2, work Lace Chart over 109 sts, yarn over (yo), k1, place marker (pm), k1, yo (corner increases), [work Chart over 19 sts, yo, k1, pm, k1, yo] twice, work Chart over 109 sts, k2—272 sts.
Row 2 K2, work Chart over 109 sts, p2, slip marker (sm), p2, [work Chart over 19 sts, p2, sm, p2] twice, work Chart over 109 sts, k2.
Row 3 K2, work Chart over 110 sts (see page 30 for working corner increases into Chart), yo, k1, sm, k1, yo, [work Chart over 21 sts, yo, k1, sm, k1, yo] twice, work Chart over 110 sts, k2—278 sts.
Row 4 K2, work Chart over 110 sts, p2, sm, p2, [Chart over 21 sts, p2, sm, p2] twice, Chart over 110 sts, k2. Keeping first and last 2 sts in garter stitch, continue working Chart and corner increases as established until 6 rows of

Chart have been worked 18 times total. Knit 4 rows, working corner increases each side of markers on RS rows as before. Bind off.

Finishing

Block to measurements, steaming generously. This will help it drape well. Make 7 tassels 5" long, and attach 1 to each corner; their weight will help the wrap hang well and stay put.

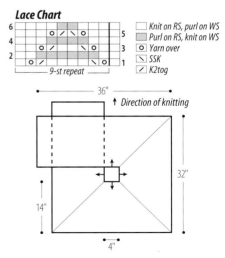

JO SHARP Jo Sharp Wool (100% wool; 50g/1¾oz; 98m/107yds) in Smoke

WORKING CORNER INCREASES INTO LACE CHART

When working increased stitches into the chart pattern, make sure that every decrease has a matching yarn over. If there are not 2 stitches over which to work a decrease, knit the stitch instead. If the yarn over of the chart falls next to the yarn over of the corner increase, omit the chart yarn over (you must omit its accompanying decrease as well). See the chart sections below for examples of both instances.

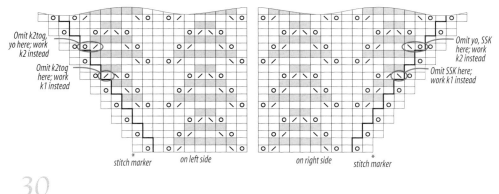

Omit k2tog, yo here; work k2 instead

Omit k2tog here; work k1 instead

*stitch marker

on left side

on right side

*stitch marker

Omit yo, SSK here; work k2 instead

Omit SSK here; work k1 instead

Diamond Wrap 10

We've combined two classic stitches, garter stitch and a modification of Barbara Walker's Afghan Stitch. Multi-directional knitting and slipped stitches are added to make a wrap that looks stylish and will keep you toasty. For an evening look, you could also knit this wrap using 'glitzy' yarns as the contrast diamonds, or add stripes in the stockinette sections.

Designed by Maureen Mason-Jamieson

Diamond Wrap

INTERMEDIATE

One size
Finished measurements (excluding tassels)
21" x 74" (beige)
23" x 80" (purple)

10cm/4"

28–30 **GET CLOSE**
20–22

• over stockinette stitch

1 2 **3-4** 5 6

• Light to Medium weight
MC • 1100 yds
CC • 275 yds

• 4mm/US6, or size to obtain gauge

• 4mm/US6, 60cm/24" long

&

• small amount of waste yarn

Notes

1 See *Techniques*, page 80, for knitted cast-on, SSK, S2KP2, and tassels. **2** Use knitted cast-on throughout. **3** Charts are on pages 33 and 34.

WRAP

Work 5 center diamonds
With straight needles and CC, cast on 25 sts. Work 24 rows of Basic Diamond Chart.
Work right half
Pick-up row (See Illustration 1.) With circular needle and MC, cast on 3 sts, then with RS of one CC diamond facing, * pick up and k12 sts along lower right edge of diamond, 1 st in point, then 12 sts along upper right edge, cast on 3 sts; repeat from * for 4 remaining diamonds—143 sts. Work Rows 1–29 of Main Pattern Chart once, then repeat Rows 6–29 eight times more. Do not cut MC.
Work 4 end diamonds
Next row (RS) (See Illustration 2.) Slip 17 sts to waste yarn, * with CC, k25, turn work and work 24 rows of Basic Diamond Chart over these 25 sts, slip next 3 MC sts to waste yarn. Repeat from * 3 times more; end last repeat by slipping last 17 sts to waste yarn.

Work edging
Begin Edging Chart
Row 1 (pick-up row) (See Illustration 3.) With RS of work facing and MC, k17 from waste yarn, pick up and k12 sts along right edge of first diamond to point, 1 st in point, then * pick up and k12 sts along left edge of diamond, k3 from waste yarn, pick up and k12 sts along right edge of next diamond, 1 st in point; repeat from * twice more, pick up and k12 sts along left edge of last diamond, k16, slip 1 with yarn in front from waste yarn—143 sts. Work through Chart Row 6. Bind off.
Work left half
Return to 5 center diamonds. With RS facing, circular needle and MC, pick up and k3 sts along 3 cast-on stitches, * pick up 25 sts along diamond as before, 3 sts along 3 cast-on stitches; repeat from * 4 times more. Work as for right half.

Finishing

Block piece. Make 8 tassels with CC, wrapping yarn 25 times around a 6" piece of cardboard. Sew tassels to points, 4 on each end.

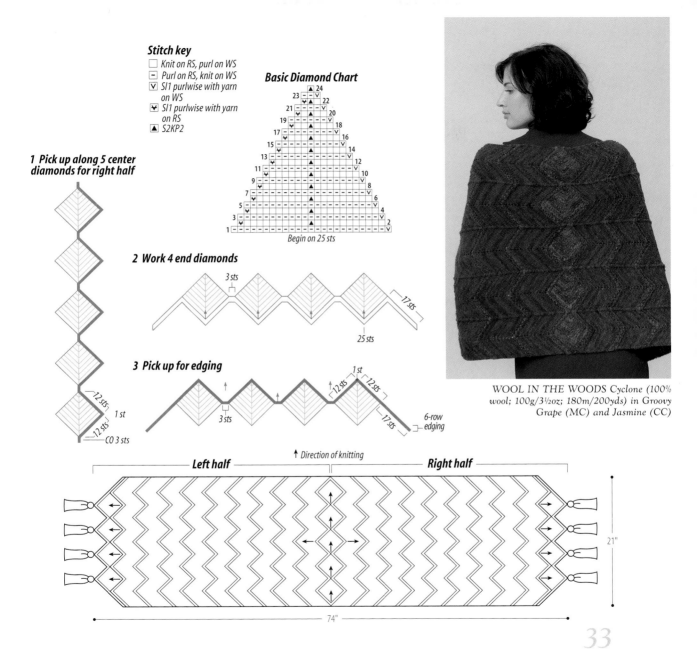

Stitch key

☐ Knit on RS, purl on WS
⊟ Purl on RS, knit on WS
☑ Sl1 purlwise with yarn on WS
☒ Sl1 purlwise with yarn on RS
▲ S2KP2

Basic Diamond Chart

Begin on 25 sts

1 Pick up along 5 center diamonds for right half

12 sts
1 st
12 sts
CO 3 sts

2 Work 4 end diamonds

3 sts
17 sts
25 sts

3 Pick up for edging

1 st
12 sts
3 sts
12 sts
17 sts
6-row edging

WOOL IN THE WOODS *Cyclone (100% wool; 100g/3½oz; 180m/200yds) in Groovy Grape (MC) and Jasmine (CC)*

← Left half —————— ↑ Direction of knitting —————— Right half →

21"

74"

33

Edging Chart

28-st repeat

Color key
- MC
- CC

Stitch key
- ☐ Knit on RS, purl on WS
- ⊟ Purl on RS, knit on WS
- ◻ SSK
- ◻ K2tog
- ✓ Sl1 purlwise with yarn on WS
- ✓ Sl1 purlwise with yarn on RS
- ▲ S2KP2
- • Pick up and knit 1 st as directed
- ✓ [K1, yo, k1] in st
- ■ Stitches do not exist in these areas of chart

Main Pattern Chart

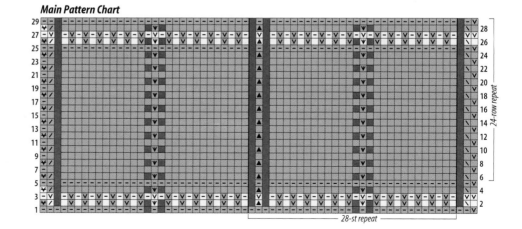

28-st repeat

24-row repeat

34

SHELRIDGE FARM Soft Touch (100% wool; 100g/3½oz; 250m/275yds) in Soft Brown (MC) and Pussywillow (CC)

11

This V-neck poncho has few limitations—throw it over a dress, bathing suit, or shorts and T-shirt for carefree spring-summer style. The lace pattern is easy, the colorway is subtle, and the look is elegant.

Designed by Kim Dolce

Flowing Sands

INTERMEDIATE

One size
Finished measurements
47½" wide × 22½" long

18cm/7"

42

29
• over Chart Pattern

1 2 3 **4** 5 6

• Medium weight
• 1530 yds

• 4.5mm/US7, or size to obtain gauge

• 3.5mm/E-4

36

Notes

1 See *Techniques,* page 80, for SSK, SK2P, yarn over (yo), fringe, single crochet (sc), and crochet chain (ch).
2 While shaping Front neck and working Chart Pattern, if a yarn over can't be paired with its corresponding decrease, omit it.

Back

Cast on 197 sts. Purl 1 row on WS.
Begin Chart Pattern: Row 1 (RS) Work 14-st repeat to last stitch, work last stitch of chart. Continue in Chart Pattern as established until 10 rows have been worked 13 times, then work Rows 1–4 once more. Piece measures approximately 22½" from beginning. Bind off.

Front

Work as for Back until 10 rows of Chart Pattern have been worked 8 times. Piece measures approximately 13½" from beginning.
Shape neck
Next row (RS) Work 98 sts, join 2nd ball of yarn and bind off center stitch, work to end. Working both sides at same time,

work as follows: Work 1 row even.
* ***Decrease row*** (RS) Work to last 3 stitches of first half, k2tog, k1; on 2nd half, k1, SSK, work to end. Work 3 rows even. Work decrease row on next row. Work 1 row even. Repeat from * 7 times more—82 sts each side. Work 4 rows even. Bind off.

Finishing

Block pieces. Sew shoulders.
Picot neck edging
With RS facing and crochet hook, begin at left shoulder and work sc along neck edge to 1 stitch before center stitch of V-neck, skip 1 stitch, sc in center stitch, skip 1 stitch, continue in sc to end.
Picot row * Work 1 sc in each of next 4 sc, ch 3, work 1 sc in same stitch as last sc worked; repeat from * around, skipping 1 stitch at center of V-neck.
Apply fringe
Cut strands of yarn to 12" lengths. Insert crochet hook from wrong side of work at lowest point of scallop. Draw center of 4 strands through, forming a loop. Pull to tighten. Repeat for each scallop of hem. Trim yarn ends even.

WOOL IN THE WOODS *Rugged (75% cotton, 21% rayon, 4% nylon; 135g/4¾oz; 80m/88yds) in Buttercream*

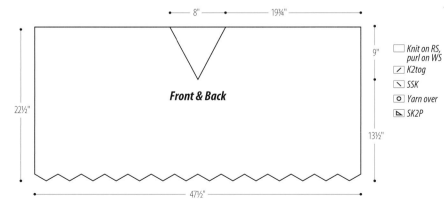

- 8" - | - 19¾" -

9"

Front & Back

22½"

13½"

47½"

☐ *Knit on RS, purl on WS*

◢ *K2tog*

◣ *SSK*

◙ *Yarn over*

◤ *SK2P*

Chart Pattern

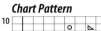

14-st repeat

37

Knit a shawl that is equally beautiful wrapped around your body or draped on a favorite easy chair. Color and texture shift as the variegated yarn stacks into garter bands arranged "log cabin" style.

Designed by Shawn Stoner

Anthracite Shawl

EASY +

One size
Finished measurements
27½" × 69"

10cm/4"

21
11
• over garter stitch
(knit every row)

1 2 3 **4** 5 6
• Medium weight
• 1300 yds

• 9mm/US13, or size to obtain gauge,
60 cm/24" long

&

• stitch marker
• waste yarn

Notes

1 See *Techniques,* page 80, for invisible cast-on. **2** Two rows of knitting equal one garter ridge.

WRAP
Section A

Invisibly cast on 10 sts. Knit 20 rows (10 garter ridges). Do not turn work. Place marker on this square to mark RS of work.

Section B

With same end of needle, pick up and k10 sts along left side of Section A. Knit 20 rows (10 ridges) over these 10 sts.

Section C

Pick up and k10 sts along left edge of Section B, then place 10 sts from cast-on edge of Section A onto other needle end, removing waste yarn, then knit these 10 sts. Knit 20 rows (10 ridges) over 20 sts.

Section D

Pick up and k10 sts along left edge of Section C, 10 sts along right edge of Section A. Knit 30 rows (15 ridges) over 20 sts.

Section E

Pick up and k15 sts along left edge of Section D, k10 sts of Section A, then pick up and k10 sts along right edge of Section B. Knit 20 rows (10 ridges) over 35 sts.

s = stitches   r = garter ridge (2 knit rows)
↑ direction of knitting

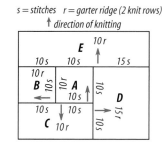

When picking up stitches along garter stitch edges, pick up in edge stitch so that wrap will be reversible.

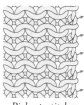

Pick up stitches along left edge   *Pick up stitches along right edge*

NORO Silk Garden (45% silk, 45% mohair, 10% wool; 50g/1¾oz; 100m/110yds) in color #72

Section F

Pick up and k10 sts along left edge of Section E, k10 sts from Section B, pick up and k10 sts along right edge of Section C. Knit 40 rows (20 ridges) over 30 sts.

Section G

Pick up and k20 sts along left edge of Section F, k20 sts from Section C, pick up and k15 sts along right edge of Section D. Knit 20 rows (10 ridges) over 55 sts.

Section H

Pick up and k10 sts along left edge of Section G, k20 sts from Section D, pick up and k10 sts along right edge of Section E. Knit 40 rows (20 ridges) over 40 sts.

Section I

Pick up and k20 sts along left edge of Section H, k35 sts from Section E, pick up and k20 sts along right edge of Section F—75 sts. Knit 35 rows (18 ridges), ending with a WS row.
Next row (RS) Bind off all stitches. Leave last bind-off stitch on right-hand needle. Do not break yarn.

Section J

Pick up and k17 sts along left edge of Section I (18 sts on right-hand needle), k30 sts from Section F, pick up and k10 sts along right edge of Section G. Work over these 58 sts as follows:
Row 1 (WS) Knit.
Row 2 Slip 1 purlwise with yarn in front, knit to end. Repeat these 2 rows 29 times more (30 ridges).

Section K

Pick up and k30 sts along left edge of Section J, k55 sts from Section G, then pick up and k20 sts along right edge of Section H—105 sts. Work as for Section I.

Section L

Pick up and k17 sts along left edge of Section K (18 sts on right-hand needle), k40 sts from Section H, pick up and k18 sts along right edge of Section I—76 sts. Knit 76 rows (38 ridges), slipping first stitch of every row. Bind off. Break yarn.

Section M

Rejoin yarn and k58 sts from Section J, then pick up and k18 sts along right edge of Section K—76 sts. Work as for Section L.

Finishing

Block piece.

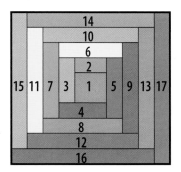

	14	
	10	
	6	
	2	
15	11	7	3	1	5	9	13	17
	4	
	8	
	12	
	16	

In the traditional log cabin quilt block, rectangles of light color alternate with rectangles of dark color to form a square. The Anthracite shawl uses one multicolored yarn and adjusts the proportion of the sections to form a rectangle.

s = stitches   r = garter ridge (2 knit rows)   ↑ direction of knitting

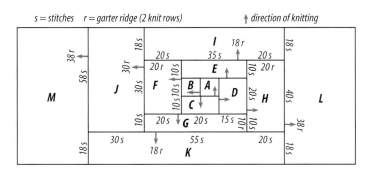

The inspiration for this little cape was a cardigan buttoned around the neck with the sleeves hanging free, worn for a bit of warmth. Since it's knit sideways it is adaptable to many sizes—to make it wider, you just knit it longer. It can also be made longer by repeating one of the cable patterns.

Designed by Wendy Sacks

Dappled Capelet

INTERMEDIATE
S–M (L–1X)
Finished measurements
Width 54½ (62½)"
Length 18¾ (18¾)"

10cm/4"

17
12½

• over stockinette stitch
(knit on RS, purl on WS)
using larger needle
• 20 sts of Chart C to 4"
• 17 sts of Chart D to 4¼"

1 2 3 4 **5** 6

• Bulky weight
• 700 (850) yds

• 5.5mm/US9 and 8mm/US11,
or sizes to obtain gauge,
74 cm/29" long

• four 20mm/¾"

• 2 cable needles (cn), stitch markers

Notes 1 See *Techniques*, page 80, for yarn over (yo). **2** Body of Cape is worked from center front to center front, then stitches are picked up for yoke.

BODY

With larger needle, cast on 74 sts. Knit 2 rows.
Foundation row 1 (RS) K3, p1, * k2, p2, k4, p2, k2, p2 *; repeat from * to * twice more, k9, p2; repeat from * to * once, k3.
Row 2 P3, * k2, p2, k2, p4, k2, p2 *, k2, p9, repeat from * to * 3 times, k4.
Begin Chart patterns: Row 1 (RS) Work 6 sts Chart A, 8 sts Chart B, 20 sts Chart C, 8 sts Chart B, 17 sts Chart D, 8 sts Chart B, 7 sts Chart E. Continue in Chart patterns as established until piece measures 53

Key

◻ Knit on RS, purl on WS

▨ Purl on RS, knit on WS

B **Make Bobble (MB)** [K1, p1, k1, p1, k1] in one st, turn; p5, pass 2nd, 3rd, 4th and 5th st, one at a time, over first st and off needle, turn; k1 through back loop

⟩⟨ **2/2 RC** Sl 2 to cn, hold to back, k2; k2 from cn

⟩⟨ **2/2 LC** Sl 2 to cn, hold to front, k2; k2 from cn

⟩⟨ **2/2 RPC** Sl 2 to cn, hold to back, k2; p2 from cn

⟩⟨ **2/2 LPC** Sl 2 to cn, hold to front, p2; k2 from cn

⟩⟨ **2/2/4 LC** Sl 2 to cn, hold to front, sl 4 to 2nd cn, hold to back; k2; k4 from 2nd cn; k2 from first cn

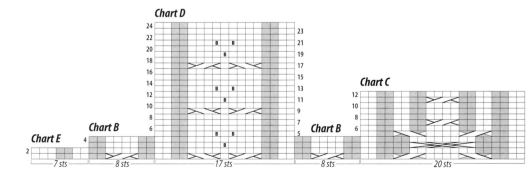

MANOS DEL URUGUAY
100% Wool (100% wool;
100g/3½oz; 124m/138yds)
in Cirrus

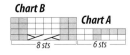

Chart B

Chart A

8 sts   6 sts

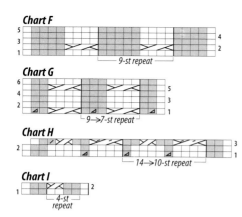

Chart F

9-st repeat

Chart G

9→7-st repeat

Chart H

14→10-st repeat

Chart I

4-st repeat

Key

- ☐ Knit on RS, purl on WS
- ▨ Purl on RS, knit on WS
- ◿ P2tog
- ◢ P3tog

⟋⟍ **1/1 RC** Sl 1 to cn, hold to back, k1; k1 from cn

⟋⟍ **2/2 RC** Sl 2 to cn, hold to back, k2; k2 from cn

⟋⟍ **2/2 dec RC** Sl 2 to cn, hold to back, k2tog; k2tog from cn

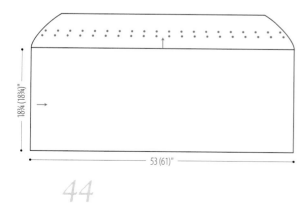

18¾ (18¾)"

53 (61)"

44

(61)" from beginning, end with a RS row. Knit 2 rows. Bind off firmly.

Yoke
With RS facing and smaller needle, pick up and k185 (203) sts evenly along edge of Chart E. Work 5 rows of Chart F. Repeat Rows 2–5 of Chart F once more. Work 6 rows of Chart G—143 (157) sts. Work 3 rows of Chart H—84 (92) sts.

Collar
Work Chart I for 2½", end with Row 2. Bind off in pattern firmly.

Finishing
Block piece.
Buttonband
With RS facing and smaller needle, pick up and k99 sts along left front edge.
Begin rib pattern: Row 1 (WS) * P1, k1; repeat from *, end p1.
Row 2 * K1, p1; repeat from *, end k1. Repeat Row 1 once more. Bind off in rib firmly.
Buttonhole Band
Place 4 markers for buttonholes along right front edge, with the first ½" from upper edge, and 3 others below first, spaced approximately 1½" apart. Work to correspond to buttonband, working buttonholes (k2tog, yarn over) at markers on 2nd rib row. Sew on buttons.

14

The simple stitch and shape of this shawl make it a good choice for "mindless" knitting. Woven-in novelty yarn gives a unique look and flair, appropriate for everyday or evening use. A short version with optional patch pockets would make a great gift for someone in a wheelchair.

Designed by Edie Eckman

Sugarplum&Toffee

it's easy
...go for it!

EASY

Short (Long) Finished measurements (excluding fringe) 66 (76)" long

10cm/4"

12

11

• over stockinette stitch (St st) with A after weaving with B, using larger needles

 1 2 3 **4** 5 6

• Medium weight
A • 665 (760) yds

1 2 3 4 **5** 6

• Bulky weight
B • 420 (490) yds

• 9mm/US13, or size to obtain gauge, 80cm/29" long

• 4mm/US6 and 9mm/US13

&

• yarn needle

To make gauge swatch

Follow instructions and make 1 pocket, including weaving but not including edging. Swatch should measure approximately 5" × 6".

Base fabric

With circular needle and A, cast on 180 (210) sts. Working back and forth, work 60 (72) rows in St st (knit on RS, purl on WS). Bind off all stitches.

Weaving

Cut lengths of B to approximately 77 (87)" long. With yarn needle, weave 1 strand of B under left-hand side of every stitch along last row of St st before bind-off, leaving approximately 5½" of B at each end for fringe. Weave another strand of B under right-hand side of each stitch on same row (see illustration). Continue in this way, weaving 2 lengths of B through each row of St st, until all rows have been woven. The base fabric will draw up as weaving continues. Smooth it out as you work to maintain width of approximately 66 (76)".

Optional pockets (make 2)

With larger straight needles and A, cast on 14 sts. Work 18 rows in St st. Bind off. Cut lengths of B and weave through stitches as for shawl, omitting fringe. At each edge of pocket, turn and continue weaving back and forth, adding new lengths of B when necessary.

Pocket edging

With smaller needles and A, pick up and k27 sts along one side edge of pocket. Work ¾" in k1, p1 rib. Bind off.

Finishing

Block piece. Tie overhand knot in each pair of fringe strands and trim to 3½". Center one pocket at each end of shawl approximately 3" from edge, with pocket edging facing center of shawl. Sew in place.

Medium weight wool in Navy (A)
CLASSIC ELITE Applause (33% mohair, 41% rayon, 14% silk, 6% wool, 6% nylon; 50g/1¾oz; 62m/70yds) in Lavender Tweed (B)

Toffee

Why not try condo knitting? A thick needle and a thin one make up the fabric. Then weave through the longer stitch rows.

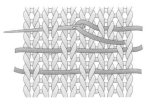

* Weave over 2 stitches, under 1 stitch; skip 1 row; move a stitch to the left and repeat from *. This loosely-woven fabric shows ribbon at its silky best.

Some yarns seem just too beautiful to use in knitting, so why not use them for surface embellishment! Ribbons are especially suited to weaving. They are smooth and glide easily through the fabric. To display a wide ribbon to best advantage, the floats can be long.

Base fabric

Work as for Sugarplum, using one large and one small needle.

Weaving

Cut B to approximately 77 (87)" lengths. With yarn needle, weave 1 strand of B in every other (longer) row of fabric as shown in illustration, leaving a tail approximately 5½" at each end for fringe. Smooth out fabric as you work to maintain width of approximately 66 (76)".

Finishing

Block piece.

Optional Knot pairs of fringe or stitch with matching sewing thread to secure ends and trim ends if you wish.

ELSEBETH LAVOLD Silky Wool (65% wool, 35% silk; 50g/1¾oz; 175m/193yds) in color 7 (A)
TRENDSETTER Segue (100% polyamide; 100g/3½oz; 110m/120yds) in color 1341 (B)

15

Update the traditional ruana silhouette with hand-dyed yarns. The fluid drape of the rayon and kid mohair fabric follows your every step. Wear this versatile accessory over a favorite pair of jeans, to work over your office dress, or drape it over your hottest little number for dancing or theater. Best of all, it is an easy knit.

Designed by Anita Tosten

Rhythm and Blues

it's easy ...go for it!

EASY
Sizes S (M, L)
Finished measurements (closed)
Underarm 44 (48, 52)"
Approximate length (stretched)
43½ (46½, 46½)"

10cm/4"

19
16

• over stockinette stitch (knit on RS, purl on WS) using 1 strand each A & B held together

1 2 3 **4** 5 6

• Medium weight
A, B • 1060 (1200, 1330) yds each

• 6mm/US10, or size to obtain gauge

&

• stitch holders

Notes
1 See *Techniques*, page 80, for SSK, 3-needle bind-off, and grafting garter stitch. **2** Work with 1 strand each A & B held together throughout. **3** To ensure even coloration, work with 2 skeins each of A & B, alternating skeins every other row. **4** Garment will stretch approximately 6–8" in length when worn. Gauge given is for unstretched fabric. Measurements on schematic indicate unstretched length.

Back
With 1 strand each A & B held together, cast on 88 (96, 104) stitches. Knit 6 rows.
Begin pattern: Row 1 (RS) Knit.
Row 2 K4, purl to last 4 sts, k4. Repeat these 2 rows 81 (88, 88) times more.
Shape neck
Next row (RS) K31 (34, 37), join new yarn and bind off 26 (28, 30) sts; knit to end. Working both sides at same time, bind off from each neck edge 2 sts once—29 (32, 35) sts each side. Work 4 rows even. Place stitches on hold.

Right Front
Cast on 44 (48, 52) sts. Work as for Back until Rows 1 and 2 of pattern have been worked 43 (50, 50) times.
Shape V-neck
Decrease row (RS) K4, SSK, knit to end. Repeat decrease row every 6th row 0 (4, 8) times, every 8th row 10 (7, 4) times— 33 (36, 39) sts. Work 3 rows even.
Next row (RS) K4 and place these stitches on hold for neckband, knit to end and place these 29 (32, 35) sts on hold.

Left Front
Work as for Right Front, reversing V-neck shaping as follows:
Decrease row (RS) Knit to last 6 sts, k2tog, k4.
Work last row as follows: K29 (32, 35) and place these stitches on hold, place remaining 4 stitches on hold for neckband. Do not cut yarn.

Finishing
Block pieces. Join 29 (32, 35) shoulder stitches each side, using 3-needle bind-off.

WOOL IN THE WOODS *Frizee (100% rayon; 100g/3½oz; 182m/200yds) in Tropical Seas (A) and Feel 'n Fuzzy (90% kid mohair/10% nylon; 100g/3½oz; 182m/200yds) in Jam Jivin' (B)*

Neckband

Row 1 (RS) Using attached yarn on Left Front band, knit into front and back (kf&b) of first stitch, knit 3—5 sts. Knit every row until neckband (slightly stretched) fits along Back neck to right shoulder, end with a RS row.

Next row (WS) K2tog, k3—4 stitches. With WS of work facing, graft stitches together with Right Front band, using garter stitch graft. Sew neckband in place along Back neck.

Toss one front over your shoulder.

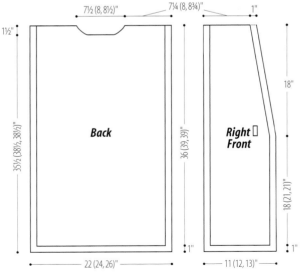

Back

Right Front

Note: *Garment will stretch approximately 6–8" in length when worn; schematic shows unstretched measurements.*

Belted, wrapped, or free-flowing,
this wrap makes a statement.

Belt it for a vest look.

Belt one front panel only.

Slip it over a
favorite dress.

16

If you've ever wanted to try entrelac but have been too intimidated, then this is the perfect first project. There's no shaping—simply knit a large rectangle, add cuffs, and sew. Entrelac is quickly mastered, and is very addictive. This shrug is the perfect accent to summer dresses, evening wear, or a casual cover-up for evening walks along the beach. You'll want to make several.

Designed by Kaleigh Young

Dramatic Datewear

INTERMEDIATE

S (M, L)
Finished measurements
Center back height 12 (15, 18)"
Length (cuff to cuff) 54½ (58, 61½)"

10cm/4"
20-22 | GET CLOSE
16-18
• over stockinette stitch
(knit on RS, purl on WS) using larger
needles and MC

1 2 3 **4** 5 6

• Medium weight
MC • 486 (486, 486) yds
CC • 380 (380, 570) yds

• 4.5mm/US7 and 5.5mm/US9, or size to
obtain gauge

• 4mm/G-6

Notes
1 See *Techniques*, page 80, for M1 knit, M1 purl, single crochet, and SSK. **2** Turn work after every row unless otherwise indicated. **3** Where instructions refer to M1, work M1 knit on RS rows and M1 purl on WS rows.

SHRUG
With larger needles and MC, cast on 32 (40, 48) sts.

Tier 1
MAKE 4 (5, 6) BASE TRIANGLES
* Row 1 (WS) P2.
Row 2 and all RS rows Knit to end of base triangle being worked.
Row 3 P3.
Row 5 P4.
Row 7 P5.
Row 9 P6.
Row 11 P7.
Row 13 P8, do not turn (one 8-st base triangle complete). Repeat from * 3 (4, 5) times more. Turn work. Cut MC.

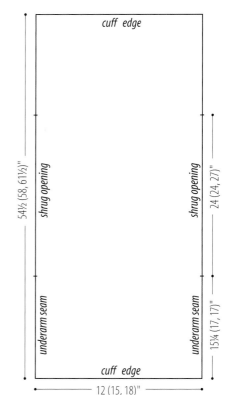

cuff edge

shrug opening

shrug opening

54½ (58, 61½)"

24 (24, 27)"

underarm seam

underarm seam

15¼ (17, 17)"

cuff edge

12 (15, 18)"

COLINETTE *Skye* (100% wool; 100g/3½oz; 150m/162yds)
COLINETTE *Hand-dyed Mohair* (78% mohair, 13% wool, 9% nylon; 100g/3½oz; 175m/190yds)

TIER 2
Work right-edge triangle, CC rectangles, and left-edge triangle.

TIER 3
Work MC rectangles.

Tier 2

WORK RIGHT-EDGE TRIANGLE

Row 1 (RS) With CC, k2.

Row 2 and all WS rows Purl.

Row 3 K1, M1, SSK (1 st of right-edge triangle together with 1 st of base triangle or MC rectangle).

Row 5 K1, M1, k1, SSK.

Row 7 K1, M1, k2, SSK.

Row 9 K1, M1, k3, SSK.

Row 11 K1, M1, k4, SSK.

Row 13 K1, M1, k5, SSK, do not turn.

WORK 3 (4, 5) CC RECTANGLES

* With RS facing, pick up and k8 sts along remaining side of base triangle (or MC rectangle).

Row 1 (WS) P8.

Row 2 K7, SSK (1 st of CC rectangle together with 1 st of base triangle or MC rectangle). Repeat Rows 1 and 2 seven times more, do not turn after last repeat. Repeat from * 2 (3, 4) times more.

WORK LEFT-EDGE TRIANGLE

With RS facing, pick up and k8 sts along remaining side of last base triangle (or MC rectangle).

Row 1 and all WS rows Purl.

Row 2 K6, k2tog.

Row 4 K5, k2tog.

Row 6 K4, k2tog.

Row 8 K3, k2tog.

Row 10 K2, k2tog.

Row 12 K1, k2tog.

Row 14 K2tog.

Cut CC and fasten off.

Tier 3

WORK 4 (5, 6) MC RECTANGLES

* With WS facing and MC, pick up and p8 sts along left-edge triangle (or CC rectangle).

Row 1 (RS) K8.

Row 2 P7, p2tog (1 st of MC rectangle together with 1 st of CC rectangle or right-edge triangle). Repeat Rows 1 and 2 seven times more, do not turn after last repeat. Repeat from * 3 (4, 5) times more. Cut MC. Turn work.

[Repeat Tiers 1 and 2] 13 (14, 15) times more, then work Tier 2 once more.

Last Tier

WORK 4 (5, 6) TOP TRIANGLES

First triangle With WS facing and MC, pick up and p8 sts along left-edge triangle.

Row 1 (RS) K8.

Row 2 P7, p2tog.

Row 3 K6, k2tog.

Row 4 P6, p2tog.

Row 5 K5, k2tog.

Row 6 P5, p2tog.

Row 7 K4, k2tog.

Row 8 P4, p2tog.

Row 9 K3, k2tog.
Row 10 P3, p2tog.
Row 11 K2, k2tog.
Row 12 P2, p2tog.
Row 13 K1, k2tog.
Row 14 P1, p2tog.
Row 15 K2tog.
Row 16 P2tog, do not turn.
Next triangle With WS facing, pick up and p8 sts along CC rectangle—9 sts.
Row 1 (RS) K7, k2tog. Repeat Rows 2–16 of first triangle. Repeat from * 2 (3, 4) times more. Fasten off last stitch.

Finishing
Block piece.
Cuffs
With RS facing, smaller needles and MC, pick up and k56 (60, 64) sts evenly along each cuff edge. Purl 1 row, decrease 10 sts evenly across—46 (50, 54) sts. Work 3" in k1, p1 rib. Bind off all stitches in rib. Sew cuff seam and underarm seam for approximately 15¼ (17, 17)". With RS facing and MC, work single crochet around shrug opening.

Color Key
◻ Dusk (MC)
◼ Velvet plum (CC)
↑ Direction of knitting
◣ Base Triangle
◀ Right-edge Triangle
◆ CC Rectangle
▶ Left-edge Triangle
◇ MC Rectangle
▽ Top Triangle

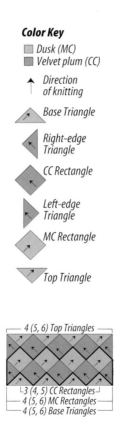

4 (5, 6) Top Triangles
Work 14 (15, 16) x
3 (4, 5) CC Rectangles
4 (5, 6) MC Rectangles
4 (5, 6) Base Triangles

NORO Silk Garden (45% silk, 45% mohair, 10% wool; 50g/1¾oz; 100m/110yds) in 86

Make it Yours!

For an easier fit over the shoulders and a longer back, enlarge the entrelac blocks by 1 stitch every 2 tiers to the shoulder. Although the color arrangement looks complex, it is just one colorway of Noro's Silk Garden doing what comes naturally. Almost—we did work one tier from the center of the ball and the next tier from the outside of the ball.

Work as original Dramatic Datewear EXCEPT work Tier 2 and 3 Triangles each for 2 more rows (9-st Triangles) and pick up and knit 9 sts instead of 8 for each Tier 2 and 3 Rectangle. Then work 10-st Triangles and Rectangles for Tiers 4 and 5, 11-st Triangles and Rectangles for Tiers 6 and 7, 12-st Triangles and Rectangles for Tiers 8 and 9 and to second shoulder.

Then repeat the graduation in reverse, working 2 tiers each on 12, 11, 10, and 9 stitches. Continue with original instructions from Top Tier.

Several tones of tweed yarn give depth and richness to this quilt-inspired design. The woven-in stranding creates a knit that behaves more like a woven fabric, perfect for an overpiece like this. Weave in the yarn ends as you go for speedy finishing. "Cufflink" buttons at the armholes keep the ruana in place.

Designed by Claire Marcus

Trapezoid Ruana

Notes
1 See *Techniques*, page 80, for Make 1 and loop cast-on. **2** When changing color before and after seed stitch border, bring new color under old to twist yarns and prevent holes. **3** Carry both colors of each row across wrong side of work; to prevent long, loopy strands, weave unused yarn above and below working yarn (see Weaving, page 63). **4** Chart and Stripe Pattern on page 63.

Seed stitch
Row 1 * K1, p1; repeat from *.
Row 2 Knit the purl stitches and purl the knit stitches. Repeat Row 2 for seed st.

Back
With 32" needle and A, cast on 104 sts. Work 5 rows in seed st and Stripe Pattern for Blues/Greens, ending with 1 row C.
Begin Chart: Row 1 (RS) Work 3 sts in seed st with C, then work 14-st repeat of chart across to last 3 sts; with C, work 3 sts in seed st.
Continue working 3 sts each side in seed st and Stripe Pattern for Blues/Greens, and remaining stitches in chart pattern,

INTERMEDIATE +

One size
Finished measurements
Width at underarm (closed) 60"
Length 29"

10cm/4"

20

14
• over chart pattern

1 2 3 **4** 5 6

• Medium weight
A, D, E, F, G, H, I • 180 yds each
B, C • 360 yds each

• 5mm/US8, or size to obtain gauge,
40cm/16" and 80cm/32" long

• eight 12mm/½"

&

• stitch holders

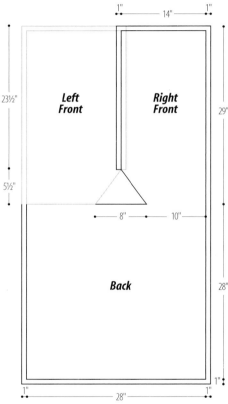

TAHKI • STACY CHARLES Donegal Homespun Tweed (100% wool; 100g/3½oz; 167m/183yds) in Olive (A), Emerald (B), Lime (C), Blue (D), Dark Gray (E), Light Gray (F), Light Brown (G), Light Tan (H), and Ecru (I).

"CUFFLINK" BUTTONS

1 Sew two buttons back to back using a knitting needle as a spacer.

2 Remove spacer and bring needle between buttons.

3 Buttonhole wrap to secure.

4 Knot end, clip for finished button.

through chart Row 84; then work chart Rows 1–56 once more. Piece measures approximately 29" from beginning.

Divide for Fronts
Shape neck

Next row (RS) Work 38 sts (Right Front); place next 28 sts on hold for neck, join new yarn, and work to end (Left Front). Working both sides at same time, work as follows: work 1 row even.

Next (increase) row (RS) Work to last stitch of Right Front, Make 1 (M1), k1; on Left Front, k1, M1, work to end. Repeat increase row (working increases into pattern) every RS row 12 times more— 51 sts each Front. Work 1 row even.

Next row (RS) Work to last stitch of right front, M1, k1, then with C, loop cast-on 3 sts for Front band; on Left Front, with C, loop cast-on 3 sts for Front band, then k1, M1, work in pattern to end—55 sts each front. Working 3 Front band stitches at each Front edge in seed st and Stripe patterns to match bands at sides, and remaining stitches in chart as established, work even until piece measures same length as Back to lower edge above seed st bands; end with chart Row 28. Work 1 row in seed st with C over all stitches, then work 2 rows with B and 2 rows with A. Bind off all stitches with A.

Finishing
With RS facing, 16" needle, and A, begin at Right Front edge and pick up and

k26 sts along Right Front neck to neck holder, k28 sts from holder, then pick up and k26 sts along Left Front neck—80 sts. Work in seed st as follows: 1 row A, 2 rows D, 1 row A.

Bind off all stitches with A. Block piece. Attach 2 clasps ("cufflinks") to each side, with the first approximately 15" below shoulder, and the second 3½" below the first.

Stripe pattern for Blues/Greens
(Seed st borders and chart)
Work in color sequence as follows: 2 rows each * A, B, C, D, C, B; repeat from *.

Color Key
- ■ Olive (A)
- ■ Emerald (B)
- ■ Lime (C)
- ■ Blue (D)
- ■ Dk. Gray (E)
- ■ Lt. Gray (F)
- ■ Lt. Brown (G)
- ■ Lt. Tan (H)
- □ Ecru (I)

Chart

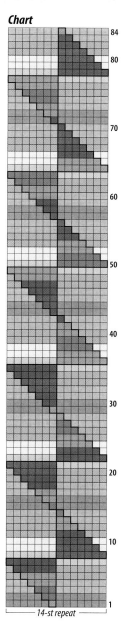

14-st repeat

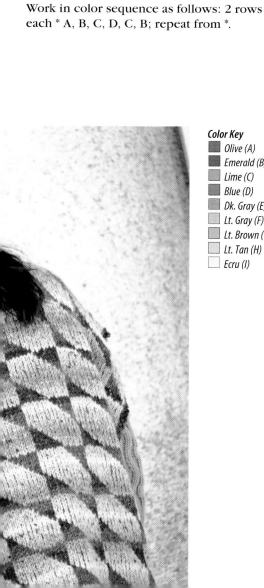

WEAVING

The unused yarn is woven alternately above and below the working yarn on the purl side of the work.

On the knit side

To weave carried yarn above a knit  stitch: Insert needle into stitch and under woven yarn, then knit the stitch as usual.

To weave carried yarn below a knit stitch: Insert needle into stitch and above woven yarn, then knit the stitch as usual.

On the purl side
To weave carried yarn above a purl stitch: Insert needle into  stitch and under woven yarn, then purl the stitch as usual.

To weave carried yarn below a purl stitch: Insert needle into  stitch and above woven yarn, then purl the stitch as usual.

The knitting is easy, although you'll need to take some care with the blocking. Like all lace, the finished appearance depends on proper blocking. For the cape, choose a yarn with luster and drape, like this lovely hand-dyed mohair blend.

Designed by Gayle Roehm

The Dawn of the Cape

EASY +

One size, three variations
BED JACKET (CAPE, CIRCLE SHAWL)
Approximate finished length 21 (28, 30)"

22
16
• over gauge swatch pattern
using larger needles

1 2 3 **4** 5 6

• Medium weight
• 480 (960, 1200) yds

• 5.5mm/US9, or size to obtain gauge,
60 cm/24" long

• 4.5mm/US7 for BED JACKET & CAPE
• One 10mm/US15 used for binding off

• four 5.5mm/US9 for CIRCLE SHAWL

☺

• three 20mm/¾" for BED JACKET & CAPE

&

• stitch markers

Notes
1 See *Techniques*, page 80, for SSK and yarn over (yo). **2** Piece is worked from the neck down. **3** Chart is on page 66.

Gauge swatch
With size 9 needles, cast on 24 sts.
Rows 1, 3, and 5 (WS) K1, p22, k1.
Row 2 K1, [(k2tog) twice, (yo, k1) 3 times, yo, (SSK) twice] twice.
Row 4 Knit.
Work Rows 2–5 five times more. Bind off. Block swatch. Width between 2 edge stitches measures 5½"; length at center of swatch (not the longest point) measures 4½".

Blocking
Note Careful wet blocking is required. The fabric wants to pucker up along the decreases, so take your time and use lots of pins and steam.
Block as follows:
1 Cover a large blocking board, bed, or carpet with a sheet or large towel. **2** Soak the finished piece in warm water, making sure it is completely wet. After a few minutes, remove and squeeze out as much water as you can without wringing. Roll in a towel to remove excess water, or spin in the washer or a salad spinner. **3** Beginning with the front and neck edges, pin the center front edges to approximately 17 (23)" long with an angle of approximately 120 degrees between them. **4** Pin the neck edge without stretching. **5** Place a pin in the shortest and longest edges of each scallop, spacing the scallops evenly around. **6** Pin the curves of each scallop into a pleasing shape. Use as many pins as you need. Take your time and adjust as necessary to even out each scallop. This is a key step for the final appearance.
7 Steam press, using a press cloth. Press the iron straight down, gently, on each section. Don't push the iron around, just lift and press down. Let dry completely.

BED JACKET & CAPE
Neckband
With smaller needles, cast on 84 sts. Knit 5 rows.
Buttonhole row (RS) Knit to last 5 sts, bind off 2 sts, knit to end.
Next row Knit, casting on 2 sts over bound-off stitches. Knit 4 rows.

MOUNTAIN COLORS *Mountain Goat*
(55% mohair, 45% wool; 113g/4oz; 219m/240yds)
in Clearwater

Chart Pattern

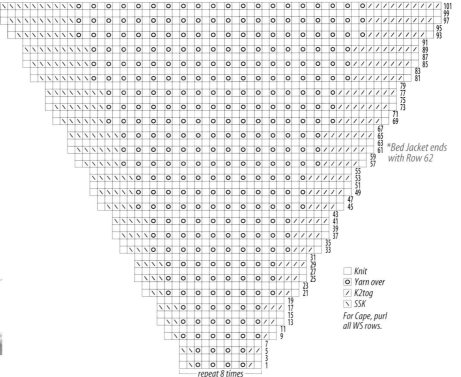

Row numbers visible: 101, 99, 97, 95, 93, 91, 89, 87, 85, 83, 81, 79, 77, 75, 73, 71, 69, 67, 65, 63, 61, 59, 57, 55, 53, 51, 49, 47, 45, 43, 41, 39, 37, 35, 33, 31, 29, 27, 25, 23, 21, 19, 17, 15, 13, 11, 9, 7, 5, 3, 1

*Bed Jacket ends with Row 62

□ Knit
⊙ Yarn over
∕ K2tog
∖ SSK

For Cape, purl all WS rows.

repeat 8 times

Body

Change to circular needle.

Begin Borders K6 sts at beginning and end of every row EXCEPT Rows 11, 12, 25, and 26, (place markers), work chart repeat over center sts as follows:

Row 1 (RS) [K1, k2tog, (yo, k1) 3 times, yo, SSK, k1] 8 times (Row 1 of Chart Pattern)—100 sts (including borders).

Row 2 and all WS rows (except 12 and 26) Purl.

Row 3 Knit.

Row 5 [(K2tog) twice, (yo, k1) 3 times, yo, (SSK) twice] 8 times.

Row 7 Knit.

Continue as established, working chart between markers on RS rows.

Row 11, all sts Repeat Buttonhole row.

Rows 12 and 26, all sts K3, cast on 2 sts, k1, purl to last 6 sts, k6.

Row 25, all sts K6, work chart repeat to last 5 sts, k1, bind off 2 sts, k to end.

Bed jacket only Skip Rows 63–102.

66

Row 102 (WS) K6, sm, purl to marker, sm, k6.

Both versions Knit 12 rows. With size 15 needle, bind off.

Note A smaller button sewn on the wrong side of the fabric underneath the fashion button can reduce the stress on a light fabric.

CIRCLE SHAWL

With dpn, cast on 12 sts, divide evenly over 3 dpn. Place marker and join, being careful not to twist sts.

Rounds 1, 2, 4, 6, 8, and 10 Knit.

Round 3 [K1, yo] 12 times—24 sts.

Round 5 [Yo, k2] 12 times—36 sts.

Round 7 [K1, (yo, k1) twice] 12 times—60 sts.

Round 9 [K2tog, yo, k1, yo, SSK] 12 times.

Round 11 [K1, (yo, k1) 4 times] 12 times—108 sts.

Knit 3 rounds.

Change to circular needle.

Begin Chart Pattern: Round 1 Work Chart repeat 12 times.

Round 2 and all even numbered rounds Knit.

Continue in Chart Pattern through Round 101.

Knit 1 round, [purl 1 round, knit 1 round] 6 times. With size 15 needle, bind off. Block as for cape. The distance from center to longest point of scallop is approximately 30".

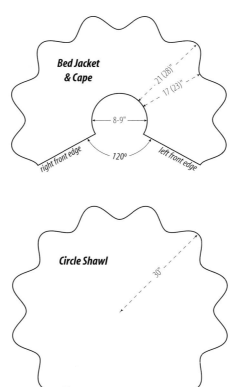

Bed Jacket & Cape

21 (28)"
17 (23)"
8-9"
right front edge
left front edge
120°

Circle Shawl

30"

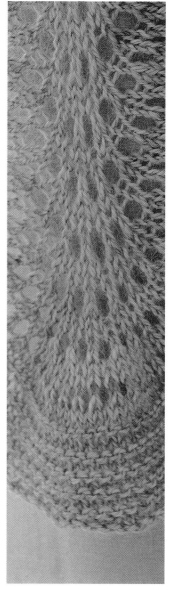

67

ADVANCED

S (M, L)
Finished measurements
Sleeve to sleeve 19 (22½, 25½)"
Diameter 51½ (51½, 51½)"

10cm/4"

17
14
• over Chart A
(see Note 6)

1 2 3 4 **5** 6

• Bulky weight
• 1650 (1870, 2200) yds

• 6mm/US10, or size to obtain gauge,
40 cm/16" long and 74 cm/29" long

• four 6mm/US10

&

• stitch holders, crochet hook, contrasting
waste yarn

This begins as a classic Elizabeth Zimmermann "Pi" shawl, all the way to the knitted-on garter stitch border. But then you add sleeves! Easy with another of EZ's inventions, the waste yarn 'thumb trick.' When you wear it, the upper edge folds back to make a lavish shawl collar. You can close it with a pin, belt it, button it, or let it drape gracefully.

Designed by Gayle Roehm

Sleeves in Your Pi

Notes

1 See *Techniques*, page 80, for SSK, S2KP2, invisible cast-on, and grafting. **2** Shawl is knit circularly from the center out. **3** Sleeve placement is marked as shawl is worked, then sleeves are worked later from the top down. **4** Change needle lengths as necessary. **5** Charts are on page 71. **6** For gauge swatch, work Rounds 1–18 of Chart A. Put stitches on a string and block piece; if gauge is OK, continue working rest of shawl.

DETERMINING YOUR SIZE

This shawl will fit better if you determine where your sleeves should start. Measure across your back, just below the shoulder blades, from the outside of one arm to the outside of the other. This number is the shawl's diameter for marking sleeve placement. The finished diameter of the shawl should approximately equal your armspan from wrist to wrist with arms held out.

19 (22½, 25½)"

Sleeve placement

51½"

SHAWL

With crochet hook, using Emily Ocker's beginning (see illustration), cast on 6 sts, divide evenly over 3 dpn. Place marker, join, and knit 1 round.
Begin Chart A: Round 1 [K1, yo] 6 times—12 sts. Continue in Chart pattern through Round 30, working Chart repeat 6 times every round—168 sts.

EMILY OCKER'S BEGINNING

Make a ring with the short end below. (This can be roomy; it will be tightened later.) **1** Chain through the ring.

2 Chain through the last chain. This is the first stitch and waits on the crochet hook.

3 Repeat Steps 1 and 2 until there are 6 loops on the hook. Distribute the loops onto 3 dpn. After working around in pattern for several inches, you may pull on the short end to close the ring.

di.Vé Mohair Kiss (73% mohair, 22% wool, 5% nylon; 50g/1¾oz; 90m/98yds)

Begin Chart B (**Note** Move round marker 1 stitch to the left at the beginning of Round 1, then every 4th round thereafter as follows: remove marker, slip 1, replace marker.)

Round 1 Move marker, [work Round 1 over 14 stitches] 12 times. Continue in Chart pattern through Round 3 (9, 15), working Chart repeat 12 times every round—192 (240, 264) sts.

Sleeve Placement

Next round *K32 (40, 44), then with waste yarn knit next 32 (40, 44) sts, return these 32 (40, 44) sts to left-hand needle and with main yarn knit them again, k32 (40, 44); repeat from* once more. Continue in Chart pattern through Round 44—432 sts. Repeat Rounds 43 and 44 two more times, or until shawl is the desired diameter (minus 4" border).

Work Border

Remove marker. Invisibly cast on 12 sts onto left-hand needle.

Begin Chart C: Row 1 (RS) Work Row 1 of Chart C over 13 sts, working last k2tog using 1 st from border and 1 st from body of shawl. Continue in Chart pattern as established until all shawl stitches have been used; end with Chart Row 15. Graft stitches together with cast-on stitches.

Sleeves

(**Note** When removing waste yarn, put sleeve stitches on 2 separate needles, then work all stitches with 16" needle.)

Gently pull out waste yarn from sleeve placement stitches, placing 32 (40, 44) loops closest to edge of shawl on 16" needle, and 32 (40, 44) loops closest to center on another needle—64 (80, 88) sts total.

Begin Sleeve Chart: Round 1 With 16" needle, begin with stitches closest to center of shawl, place marker, [work Chart Round 1 over 16 (20, 22) sts] 4 times. Continue in Chart pattern until sleeve measures 14" from beginning.

Work Border

Work as for body.

Finishing

Block shawl, pinning out each point of border. Steam heavily and let dry.

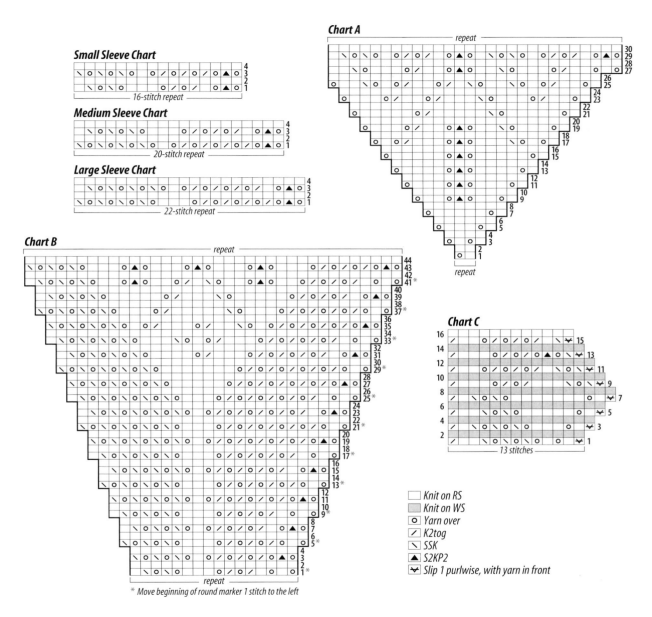

Small Sleeve Chart

16-stitch repeat

Medium Sleeve Chart

20-stitch repeat

Large Sleeve Chart

22-stitch repeat

Chart A

repeat

Chart B

repeat

* Move beginning of round marker 1 stitch to the left

Chart C

13 stitches

☐ Knit on RS
▨ Knit on WS
◉ Yarn over
╱ K2tog
╲ SSK
▲ S2KP2
↩ Slip 1 purlwise, with yarn in front

71

Mohair allows the knitter to loosen up the gauge for faster knitting and better drape. This interesting shape is formed via different increase spacings: however, it's still very easy, mostly in garter stitch. The eyelets underscore the direction and shape of the knitting.

Designed by Lily M. Chin

Dramatic Drape Update

it's easy ...go for it!

EASY +

One size
Finished measurements (excl. fringe)
Width 70"
Length 31"

10cm/4"
20
11

• over garter stitch (knit every row)

1 2 3 **4-5** 6

• Medium to Bulky weight
• 810 yds

• 8mm/US11, or size to obtain gauge,
60cm/24" long

&

• stitch markers

Increase 2 (Inc 2)
[K1, yarn over (yo), k1] into a stitch. This increase is shown on page 74.

Notes
1 See *Techniques*, page 80, for yarn-overs (yo) and fringe. *2* For ease in knitting, mark right side (RS) of work.

SHAWL
Make a slipknot on needle. Into this stitch, work [k1, yo] twice, k1—5 sts.
Row 1 (RS) Yo, k2, Inc 2, k2—8 sts.
Row 2 and all WS rows Yo, knit to end.
Row 3 Yo, k4, Inc 2, k4—12 sts.
Row 5 Yo, k6, Inc 2, k6—16 sts.
Continue in this way, working 2 more sts before and after the Inc 2 on each RS row until last row worked is yo, k90, Inc 2, k90—184 sts.
Eyelet row (WS) Yo, p1, * yo, p2tog; repeat from * to last stitch, p1—185 sts.
Shape lower center triangle
Row 1 (RS) Yo, k91, place marker, knit into front and back of next stitch (kf&b), k1, kf&b, place marker, knit to end—188 sts.
Row 2 Yo, knit to end.
Row 3 Yo, knit to marker, slip marker, kf&b, knit to 1 st before next marker,

kf&b, slip marker, knit to end.
Repeat Rows 2 and 3 until piece measures 5" from eyelet row; end with a RS row. Work eyelet row. [Work Row 3, then Row 2] 3 times, then Row 3 once. Work eyelet row. Work Row 3, then Row 2. Bind off loosely.

Finishing
Block.

Fringe
Work one 8-strand, 6" fringe section in each eyelet along lower edge. Trim as necessary.

CLASSIC ELITE La Gran (76% mohair, 18% wool, 6% nylon; 42g/1½oz; 82m/90yds) in 6526 Tidal Pool

31"

70"

Influenced by the girl's poncho in the movie "My Big Fat Greek Wedding," we introduce the new generations to a style that was so popular in the '70s. We even chose colors that are a bit bohemian, to pay homage to those simpler times.

Designed by Joni Coniglio

Retro Poncho

INTERMEDIATE

Children 4–6 (8–10, 12–14)
Adult [S (L)]

Circumference at base of neck 14 (15, 16)
[20 (26)]"
Length to lower point 14 (16½, 20¼)"
[24 (28)]"

10cm/4"

22

18

• over stockinette stitch
(knit every round) using larger needle

1 2 3 5 6

• Medium weight
MC • 195 (390, 590) [830 (950)] yds
A, B, C, D • 50 (80, 120) [170 (190)] yds
each color

• 4.5mm/US7, 16" and 32" long
• 5mm/US8, or size to obtain gauge,
16" and 32" long

• 5.5mm/I-9

&

• stitch marker

Seed Stitch Pattern

Worked circularly over an odd number of stitches.
Round 1 * K1, p1; repeat from *, end k1. ***Round 2*** * P1, k1; repeat from *, end p1. Repeat Rounds 1 and 2 for seed st.

PONCHO
Neckband

With smaller needle (16" long) and A, cast on 57 (61, 65) [109 (121)] sts. Place marker, join, and work in seed st as follows: 3 rounds A, 2 rounds B, 1 round C, 2 rounds B, 3 rounds D, 1 round MC. Change to larger needle (16" long). Continue with MC only.

Body

Next round SSK, knit to end—56 (60, 64) [108 (120)]sts.
Begin increase rounds: Round 1 * K13 (14, 15) [26 (29)], Inc 2 in next stitch; repeat from * 3 times more—64 (68, 72) [116 (128)] sts.
Round 2 and all even-numbered rounds Knit.
Round 3 K14 (15, 16) [27 (30)], Inc 2, * k15 (16, 17) [28 (31)], Inc 2; repeat from * 2 times more, k1—72 (76, 80) [124 (136)] sts.
Round 5 K15 (16, 17) [28 (31)], Inc 2, * k17 (18, 19) [30 (33)], Inc 2; repeat from * 2 times more, k2—80 (84, 88) [132 (144)] sts.
Round 7 K16 (17, 18) [29 (32)], Inc 2, * k19 (20, 21) [32 (35)], Inc 2; repeat from * 2 times more, k3—88 (92, 96) [140 (152)] sts.

LION BRAND Wool·Ease (80% acrylic, 20% wool; 85g/3oz; 180m/197yds) in Chestnut Heather (MC), Gold (A), Peacock (B), Cranberry (C), and Copper (D)

Inc 2 [k1, yo, k1] into a stitch

1 K1, leave stitch on left-hand needle, bring yarn to front (as shown) …

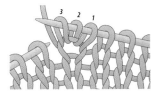

… then knit the same stitch again.

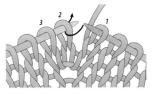

2 On next increase round, work Inc 2 into center stitch of previous increase round increase.

Round 9 K17 (18, 19) [30 (33)], Inc 2, * k21 (22, 23) [34 (37)], Inc 2; repeat from * 2 times more, k4—96 (100, 104) [148 (160)] sts. Continue to increase 8 sts every other round (work one more knit stitch before first increase and after last increase, and 2 more knit stitches between increases on every increase round) until there are 248 (284, 336) [460 (560)] sts, ending with Round 47 (55, 67) [87 (109)].

Next Round K36 (41, 48) [69 (83)], M1, * k62 (71, 84) [115 (140)], M1; repeat from * 2 times more, k25 (29, 35) [45 (56)], M1, k1—253 (289, 341) [465 (565)] sts. Change to smaller needle (32" long). Cut MC.

Lower Band
Continue in seed st and increase rounds as follows:

Round 1 With D, begin with p1, work 38 (43, 50) [71 (85)] sts in seed st, Inc 2, * begin with k1 (p1, k1) [p1 (p1)], work 62 (71, 84) [115 (140)] sts in seed st, Inc 2 *, begin with p1 (p1, p1) [p1 (k1)], work 62 (71, 84) [115 (140)] sts in seed st, Inc 2, repeat from * to * once, begin with p1 (p1, p1) [p1 (k1)], work 25 (29, 35) [45 (56)]sts in seed st—261 (297, 349) [473 (573)]sts.

Round 2 With D, begin with k1, work seed st to end.

Round 3 With D, begin with p1, work 39 (44, 51) [72 (86)] sts in seed st, Inc 2, * begin with p1 (k1, p1) [k1 (k1)], work 64 (73, 86) [117 (142)] sts in seed st, Inc 2 *, begin with k1 (k1, k1) [k1 (p1)], work 64 (73, 86) [117 (142)]sts in seed st, Inc 2, repeat from * to * once, begin with k1 (k1, k1) [k1 (p1)], work 26 (30, 36) [46 (57)] sts in seed st—269 (305, 357) [481 (581)] sts.

Round 4 With A, repeat Round 2.

Round 5 With A, begin with p1, work 40 (45, 52) [73 (87)] sts in seed st, Inc 2, * begin with k1 (p1, k1) [p1 (p1)], work 66 (75, 88) [119 (144)] sts in seed st, Inc 2 *, begin with p1 (p1, p1) [p1 (k1)], work 66 (75, 88) [119 (144)] sts in seed st, Inc 2, repeat from * to * once, begin with p1 (p1, p1) [p1 (k1)], work 27 (31, 37) [47 (58)] sts in seed st—277 (313, 365) [489 (589)] sts.

Round 6 With B, repeat Round 2.

Round 7 With B, begin with p1, work 41 (46, 53) [74 (88)] sts in seed st, Inc 2, * begin with p1 (k1, p1) [k1 (k1)], work 68 (77, 90) [121 (146)] sts in seed st, Inc 2 *, begin with k1 (k1, k1) [k1 (p1)], work 68 (77, 90) [121 (146)] sts in seed st, Inc 2, repeat from * to * once, begin with k1 (k1, k1) [k1 (p1)], work 28 (32, 38) [48 (59)] sts in seed st—285 (321, 373) [497 (597)] sts.

Round 8 With C, repeat Round 2. Continue in seed st, working increases every other round, in the following color sequence: 2 rounds B, 2 rounds C, 1 round D, 1 round A, 2 rounds C, 2 rounds B, 1 round C, 2 rounds B, 3 rounds A, 2 rounds D—357 (393, 445) [569 (669)] sts. Bind off with D.

Finishing
Block piece.

Make fringe

Cut 5 strands of yarn (1 of each color), 9" long. Holding all 5 strands together, fold them in half and with crochet hook draw center of strands through 1 st at lower edge of poncho; draw ends through loop and tighten. Work fringe around entire lower edge of poncho.

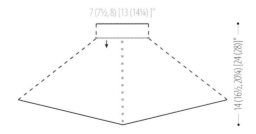

7 (7½, 8) [13 (14¼)]"

14 (16½, 20¼) [24 (28)]"

Shapes that Wrap)

Three of these 4 wraps are rectangles. No pattern needed! Find a yarn (or several), swatch for gauge and to settle on a stitch or two, then just cast on and knit. It's as easy as knitting a scarf!

Designed by Knitter's Design Team

Shapes that Wrap

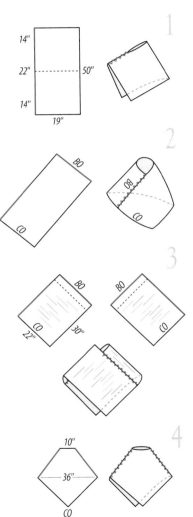

1 Purple waterfall Work rectangle in stockinette stitch, 13" wide, using waterfall cast-on and bind-off (see page 10) for a finished width of 19". Fold rectangle in half. Seam side, leaving 11" opening for neck.

2 Pink/gray Work rectangle in desired stitch pattern and yarns. Seam bind-off edge to side edge to create neck opening (see drawing). When worn, this shape has only one point (to front or back or side). Sample was knit in garter and elongated stitches.

3 Wool bouclé Knit two rectangles, each 22 × 30". Join bind-off of first piece to side edge of second, then join bind-off of one piece to side edge of the other.

4 Black diamond Knit two diamonds as follows: Cast on 3 sts. Work in garter stitch, increasing 1 stitch at beginning of every row until 36" wide (or desired width). Then decrease 1 stitch at beginning of every row until 10" remain on needle. Bind off loosely. Seam at decreased edges.

Elongated Stitch

K1, wrapping yarn 2 times (instead of once) around needle. On next row, purl (or knit) the stitch, dropping all the wraps.

3

4

1

Techniques

CAST-ONS

Knitted cast-on

1 Make a slipknot on left needle.

2 Working into this knot's loop, knit a stitch and place it on left needle.

Repeat Step 2 for each additional stitch.
If adding to existing stitches, hold needle with stitches in left hand and work Step 2 for each additional stitch.

Invisible cast-on

1 Knot working yarn to contrasting waste yarn. With needle in right hand, hold knot in right hand. Tension both strands in left hand; separate the strands with fingers of the left hand. Yarn over with working yarn in front of waste strand.

2 Holding waste strand taut, pivot yarns and yarn over with working yarn in back of waste strand.

3 Each yarn-over forms a stitch. Alternate yarn-over in front and in back of waste strand for required number of stitches. For an even number, twist working yarn around waste strand before knitting the first row. Later, untie knot, remove waste strand, and arrange bottom loops on needle.

Loop cast-on

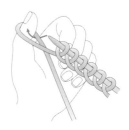

Used to cast on a few stitches. Can be worked over thumb or finger.

PICK UP AND KNIT

Stitches being picked up into first stitch , 3 stitches for every 4 rows.

For a firmer edge, pick up 1 stitch in from edge.

MISCELLANEOUS

Knit through back loop (tbl)

1 Insert the needle into the stitch from right to left.

2 Knit.

INCREASES

Make 1 knit (M1, M1K)

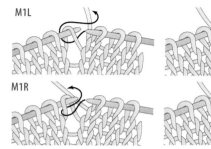

M1L

M1R

Make 1 purl (M1P)

Work as for M1L or M1R, EXCEPT *purl* into the loop.

Yarn over (yo)

Before a knit With yarn in front of needle, knit next stitch.

Before a purl With yarn in front of needle, bring yarn over needle and to front again, purl next stitch.

For a left-slanting increase (M1L)
With left needle from front of work, pick up strand between last stitch knitted and next stitch. Knit, twisting the strand by working into the loop at the back of the needle.

For a right-slanting increase (M1R)
With left needle from back of work, pick up strand between last stitch knitted and next stitch. Knit, twisting the strand by working into the loop at the front of the needle.

Lifted increase

Right lifted increase
Knit into right loop of stitch in row below next stitch on left needle (1).

Left lifted increase
Knit into left loop of stitch in row below last stitch knitted (1).

ABBREVIATIONS

CC contrasting color
cn cable needle
cm centimeter(s)
dec decreas(e)(ed)(es)(ing)
dpn double-pointed needle(s)
g gram(s)
" inch(es)
inc increas(e)(ed)(es)(ing)
k knit(ting)(s)(ted)
LH left-hand
M1 Make one stitch (increase)
m meter(s)
mm millimeter(s)
MC main color
oz ounce(s)
p purl(ed)(ing)(s) or page
pm place marker
psso pass slipped stitch(es) over
RH right-hand
RS right side(s)
sc single crochet
sl slip(ped)(ping)
SKP slip, knit, psso
SSK slip, slip, knit these 2 sts tog
SSP slip, slip, purl these 2 sts tog
st(s) stitch(es)
St st stockinette stitch
tbl through back of loop(s)
WS wrong side(s)
wyib with yarn in back
wyif with yarn in front
yd(s) yard(s)
yo(2) yarn over (twice)

BIND-OFFS

3-needle bind-off

Ridge on RS

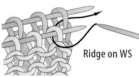

Ridge on WS

For bind-off ridge on RS
1 With stitches on 2 needles, place wrong sides together and right side facing you. * K2tog (1 from front needle and 1 from back needle); repeat from * once.

2 Pass first stitch on right needle over 2nd stitch. Continue to k2tog (1 front stitch and 1 back stitch) and bind off across.

For bind-off ridge on WS
Work Steps 1 and 2 but with right sides together and wrong side facing.

81

JOINS

Mattress stitch

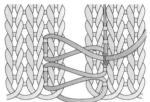

1 After blocking, thread blunt needle with matching yarn.
2 Working with right sides facing, pick up 2 bars between edge stitch and next stitch.
3 Cross to matching place in opposite piece, and pick up 2 bars.
4 Return to first piece, go down into the hole you came out of, and pick up 2 bars.
5 Return to opposite piece, go down into the hole you came out of, and pick up 2 bars.
Repeat Steps 4 and 5 across, pulling thread very tight, then stretching the seam slightly.

Grafting garter stitch

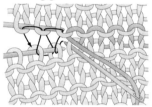

1 Arrange stitches on two needles so stitches on one needle come out of purl bumps (lower needle) and stitches on the other needle come out of smooth knits (upper needle).
2 Thread a blunt needle with matching yarn (approximately 1" per stitch).
3 Working from right to left, with right sides facing you, begin with Steps 3a and 3b:
3a Front needle: yarn through 1st stitch as if to purl, leave stitch on needle.
3b Back needle: yarn through 1st stitch as if to knit, leave on.
4 Work 4a and 4b across:
4a Front needle: through 1st stitch as if to knit, slip off needle; through next st as if to purl, leave on needle.
4b Work as 4a on back needle.
5 Adjust tension to match rest of knitting.

Grafting stockinette

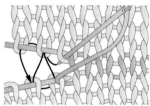

1 Arrange stitches on 2 needles.
2 Thread a blunt needle with matching yarn (approximately 1" per stitch).
3 Working from right to left, with right sides facing you, begin with Steps 3a and 3b:
3a Front needle: yarn through 1st stitch as if to purl, leave stitch on needle.
3b Back needle: yarn through 1st stitch as if to knit, leave stitch on needle.
4 Work 4a and 4b across:
4a Front needle: through 1st stitch as if to knit, slip off needle; through next st as if to purl, leave on needle.
4b Back needle: through 1st stitch as if to purl, slip off needle; through next st as if to knit, leave on needle.
5 Adjust tension to match rest of knitting.

EMBELLISHMENTS

Fringe

Cut strands of yarn to lengths as instructed. Insert crochet hook from wrong side through a stitch at edge of work. Draw center of strands through, forming a loop. Draw ends through loop. Trim yarn ends even. One fringe section completed.

Tassels

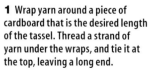

1 Wrap yarn around a piece of cardboard that is the desired length of the tassel. Thread a strand of yarn under the wraps, and tie it at the top, leaving a long end.

2 Cut the lower edge to free the wrapped strands. Wrap the long end of the yarn around the upper edge and insert the yarn into the top as shown. Trim the strands.

DECREASES

SSK

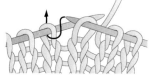

1 Slip 2 stitches separately to right needle as if to knit.

2 Knit these 2 stitches together by slipping left needle into them from left to right.

Completed: 2 stitches become one.

SSSK

Work same as SSK except:
1 Slip 3 stitches separately to right needle as if to knit.
2 Knit these 3 stitches together by slipping left needle into them from left to right; 3 stitches become one.

S2KP2, SSKP, sl2-k1-p2sso

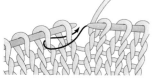

1 Slip 2 stitches together to right needle as if to knit.

2 Knit next stitch.

3 Pass 2 slipped stitches over knit stitch and off right needle.

4 Completed: 3 stitches become 1; the center stitch is on top.

P2tog

Purl 2 stitches together; 2 stitches become one.

SK2P, sl1-k2tog-psso

1 Slip one stitch knitwise.
2 Knit next two stitches together.
3 Pass the slipped stitch over the k2tog.

CROCHET

Single crochet (sc) Work slip stitch to begin.

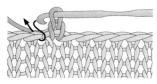

1 Insert hook into next stitch.

2 Yarn over and through stitch; 2 loops on hook.

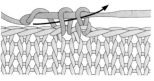

3 Yarn over and through both loops on hook; single crochet completed. Repeat Steps 1–3.

Crochet chain (ch)

Make a slipknot to begin.
1 Yarn over hook, draw yarn through loop on hook.

2 First chain made. Repeat Step 1.

Specifications:

INTERMEDIATE
One size
20" circumference x 9" deep

Skill level
Size

10cm/4"

27

21
over stockinette stitch
(k on RS, p on WS)

Gauge
The number of stitches and
rows you need in 10 cm or
4", worked as specified.

1 2 3 **4** 5 6

Medium weight
MC, A, B, C, D, E, F • 88yds each

Yarn weight
and amount in yards

Four 4.5mm/US7 double-pointed needles
(dpn) or size to obtain gauge

Type of needles
Straight, unless circular or
double-pointed
are recommended.

4.5mm/US7 circular 40cm (16") long

&

Stitch marker, yarn needle

Any extras

Conversion chart

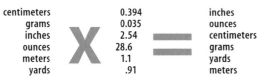

centimeters	0.394	inches
grams	0.035	ounces
inches	2.54	centimeters
ounces	28.6	grams
meters	1.1	yards
yards	.91	meters

Needles/Hooks

US	MM	HOOK
0	2	A
1	2.25	B
2	2.75	C
3	3.25	D
4	3.5	E
5	3.75	F
6	4	G
7	4.5	7
8	5	H
9	5.5	I
10	6	J
10½	6.5	K
11	8	L
13	9	M
15	10	N
17	12.75	

At a Glance

Locate the Yarn Weight and Stockinette Stitch Gauge Range over 10cm to 4" on the chart. Compare that range with the information on the yarn label to find an appropriate yarn. These are guidelines only for commonly used gauges and needle sizes in specific yarn categories.

Equivalent weights

¾	oz		20 g
1	oz		28 g
1½	oz		40 g
1¾	oz		50 g
2	oz		60 g
3½	oz		100 g

Yarn weight categories

Yarn Weight

1	2	3	4	5	6
Super Fine	Fine	Light	Medium	Bulky	Super Bulky

Also called

Sock Fingering Baby	Sport Baby	DK Light-Worsted	Worsted Afghan Aran	Chunky Craft Rug	Bulky Roving

Stockinette Stitch Gauge Range 10cm/4 inches

27 sts to 32 sts	23 sts to 26 sts	21 sts to 24 sts	16 sts to 20 sts	12 sts to 15 sts	6 sts to 11 sts

Recommended needle (metric)

2.25 mm to 3.25 mm	3.25 mm to 3.75 mm	3.75 mm to 4.5 mm	4.5 mm to 5.5 mm	5.5 mm to 8 mm	8 mm and larger

Recommended needle (US)

1 to 3	3 to 5	5 to 7	7 to 9	9 to 11	11 and larger

Sizing
Measure around the fullest part of your bust/chest to find your size.

Children	2	4	6	8	10	12	14
Actual chest	21"	23"	25"	26.5"	28"	30"	31.5"

Women	XXS	XS	Small	Medium	Large	1X	2X	3X
Actual bust	28"	30"	32–34"	36–38"	40–42"	44–46"	48–50"	52–54"

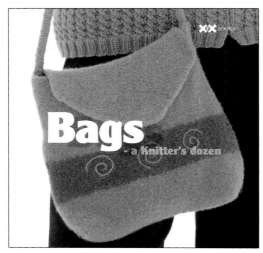

Bags
- a Knitter's dozen

XRX BOOKS

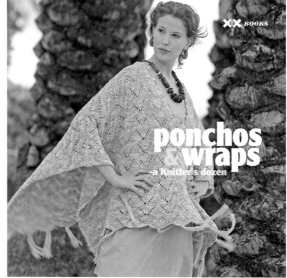

ponchos
& wraps
- a Knitter's dozen

XRX BOOKS

Scarves
-a Knitter's dozen

XX BOOKS

And more on the way!

Find them at a knit shop near you...
www.knittinguniverse.com

XX BOOKS

Hats
-a Knitter's dozen

Contributors

Kathy Cheifetz

Lily M. Chin

Joni Coniglio

Linda Cyr

Kim Dolce

Edie Eckman

Mary Rich Goodwin

Dee Jones

Claire Marcus

Maureen Mason-Jamieson

Rick Mondragon

Sue Kay Nelson

Gayle Roehm

Wendy Sacks

Gitta Schrade

Shawn Stoner

Anita Tosten

Kaleigh Young